COMMUNITIES OF THE FUTURE

COMMUNITIES OF THE FUTURE

TALES FROM SUFFOLK IN 2030

STEPHEN AND JOANNE AGUILAR-MILLAN

DESIGN BY ACCIDENT PRESS 2015

First published 2015 by the Design By Accident Press, a division of Design By Accident Limited.

ISBN: 978-0-9932322-0-6

Design By Accident Press
6 Greenways Close
Ipswich
IP1 3RB
United Kingdom

www.eufo.org

Table of Contents

CHAPTER 1

THE COMMUNITIES OF THE FUTURE

It seems that an inherent part of the human condition is a desire to unlock the unknown. This has lead humanity, through the development of the physical sciences, to gain an increasing understanding of the world in which we live. Our desire to know what is beyond our immediate horizon inspired the great voyages of discovery, which had the effect of unifying the world as a geographical entity. The curiosity about what lies beyond our planet has led to our first tentative steps into space. It is this desire to unlock the unknown that causes us to want to know what the future might hold for us.

Although we are anchored in the present, with the past determining the route upon which we have travelled, we can anticipate what future paths may be open to us. The role of the futurist in this quest is to help to understand some of the uncertainties and unknown elements that exist in this anticipation of what lies ahead. When we gaze into the future beyond our immediate horizon, it is helpful to have some sort of compass from which we can find our bearings. The role of the compass is to help us to determine which path we ought to take in order to get to our destination. It allows us to chart our way into the future, highlighting potential obstacles ahead, possible dead-ends, and those avenues that could provide us with the greatest success. The role of the futurist is to act as the compass in charting the future.

There are two important points to note here. The first is that we have determined what our destination ought to be. In terms of foresight, we would say that we have a vision of the end state that we wish to achieve. Of course, it is entirely possible that we may not have a vision of the end state that we are trying to achieve. In which case, it is usually helpful to have a vision of what a possible number of end states might be. Such visioning is

1

necessarily subjective in that the vision of one person is unlikely to be completely the same as the vision of another. This being the case, in order to achieve a given vision of the future, one person will have to persuade others of the merits of that future, if they wish to enlist the help of those people in building that future.

It is quite unlikely that any one person would be able to build a comprehensive future on their own. We all rely and interact with each other to a greater or lesser degree. Indeed, one could argue that one of our triumphs is that we have the ability to progress from the family to the tribe, from the tribe to the community, from the community to the nation, and from the nation to humanity. What binds us together in these human groupings is our shared vision of the past, present, and future – what some might call our civilisation.

This leads on to the second point to note. Even if we have determined our collective goal, there could be any number of means by which it is attained. To have decided upon the end state that we wish to acquire does not necessarily mean that we have reached a consensus about the path by which we will acquire that end state. There will always be some objections to the means by which the ends are attained. This is what strategic planning is all about, and defines the second aspect of foresight.

It could be argued that politics is the means by which we settle our differences about how a commonly shared vision of an end state is achieved. If we think of this in terms of geography, it is like saying that if we all want to go to a common destination then we need to agree upon the mode of transport and the route by which we get there. The vision is our common agreement of the destination, and politics is the means by which we decide to go by car, or train, or bus, or whatever means of transport is finally used and whichever route is taken. This brings out the point that the strategic planning aspect of foresight is also necessarily subjective.

It is our view that foresight is all about visioning and planning, both of which are subjective expressions of a common view of what the future should be and how we should attain it. Not all authorities would agree on this point. There are those who might argue that foresight should be a bit more technocratic, a bit more objective about the future likely to unfold. We do not agree with this view because we are of the opinion that no statement about the future can be made with complete certainty, which has the implication that all foresight is necessarily subjective. This is the assumption that we shall hold in this book.

There is also a mistaken belief, which is widely held, that, as the future is not perfectly knowable, and as we are unable to foresee it with any degree of certainty, there is no value to be had from foresight activities. We accept the premise, but not the conclusion drawn from the premise. It is true that we cannot foresee, with any perfect sense of certitude, how the future will unfold. That does not mean that we ought not to try to anticipate how a range of futures might unfold. If we failed to do so, then we would be blindly stumbling into the future from the present. Our lives would have no direction and certainly no meaning. One could argue that one of the major problems facing industrialised societies at present is that a large number of a rapidly aging cohort – the Baby Boomers – has failed to adequately provide for their latter years. This is an example of a failure of foresight on their part that inversely highlights the benefits of foresight.

Strangely enough, it is the uncertainty about future events that explains why we are concerned about the future. If we had perfect knowledge about future events, then we could lay our plans with complete certainty. Planning for the future would become a technocratic exercise where mathematical models could highlight for us the best course of action. It is the introduction of uncertainty about how events will unfold that causes us to want to know what different possibilities lay ahead for us.

As we can see, from the perspective of any given point in time, there are a very large number of possibilities that lay open to us in the future. Within the totality of the possible futures that may be open to us, we will find some more persuasive than others. One of the lenses through which we view possible futures is their plausibility. It has to be conceded that, on occasions, it is the implausible futures that actually happen. To many people, with some notable exceptions, the financial crash of 2007 represented an implausible future. With the benefit of hindsight, we can see now how it happened, but, before the event, although a number of commentators were warning of it, they were regarded as having outlined a future that was too implausible. There is a place for implausible futures, and that is the world of the wild card futures, which are future events of a very low probability and a very high impact. However, because of their very low probability, they have very little traction in a policy framework because it is very difficult to expect the unexpected. For our purposes, we shall keep to futures that are reasonably plausible.

Even with implausible futures being excluded, at any point in time there is still a very large range of futures that are plausible and possible. Our task is one of sifting through that range of futures to uncover a number that we find relatively convincing. We are helped in our task if we can discern a baseline future. This is what we can reasonably expect to happen in the future if no key factors change. This gives us a vision of how we see things developing. This presents us with something of a challenge. Key factors do change, and we ought to develop a view of how things might look if one or more of those factors were to change in one way or another. As we do this, we begin to create a number of possible and plausible visions of the future.

Whilst these may be possible and plausible futures, it does not mean that they are desirable futures. The desirability of that future vision adds another dimension to our task. It is entirely possible to develop a set of future visions – or scenarios, as they are often known – that are completely undesirable. Perhaps the largest set of undesirable scenarios that is

4

currently under construction is the collection of climate change scenarios. We can reasonably believe that our climate is changing. We can reasonably conclude that it is due to the impact of human activity upon the climate. We can foresee all sorts of disastrous consequences if our activities continue unchecked. So what is the purpose of these undesirable future scenarios?

This question strikes at the heart of why we study the future. The purpose of producing future scenarios is twofold. On the one hand, we develop dystopian scenarios to act as a warning about how the future could unfold, and how we could find ourselves in an undesirable position in the future if we did nothing to check this course of events. Many climate scenarios fit into this category. There is also a positive use of scenarios to counteract this negative use. A set of positive scenarios – utopian scenarios, we like to call them – can be used to inspire us to build a better future. They can help us to develop a vision of a future state of events that we really want to happen, and then to help us build that better future.

It could be objected that this is all very subjective, and we would accept that comment. Indeed, we would strengthen it further by taking the view that all futures are subjective. Much of the study of the future relates to actions that we ought to take in the present if we are to achieve our desired future. It is important to note the action element to the study of the future. The study element is not passive, it is for a purpose, and that purpose is to act to build a better future, however it is defined. This is one of the features that distinguish future scenarios from science fiction. Science fiction is entirely passive, whereas future scenarios are a prelude to action. How we ought to act is a purely subjective question. That is why we cannot say that a set of scenarios is 'right' or 'wrong'. We can only say that we find them convincing or unconvincing. They either inspire us to take a course of action, or they do not.

Examining the future is about providing a link from the present to the future. It is about inspiring people to build a better future and about warning people about the undesirable futures that we could sleepwalk into if we did not actively manage our fate. A good set of future scenarios will help people to determine what they need to do to build the future that they want. It is entirely possible that the baseline future could be perfectly desirable, in which case people will have to do nothing other than make sure that present circumstances remain in place. This is unlikely because even if we stand still, the world is changing around us, and we need to account for those changes.

It is highly unlikely, though, that all of a given group of people will see the baseline future as one that is highly desirable. The process of politics is one that gives rise to voices of discontent. It is the mechanism by which communities and nations give form to the vision of the future that they see as the most desirable, the one which they collectively want to build. This provides the process by which we engage with the future.

When we produce a number of future scenarios, we go through a process of telling a story of how the future could be. It is important to note at the outset that a key skill in setting out our visions of the future – be they utopian or dystopian – is that of storytelling. In that process, we embody our hopes and desires as well as our concerns and fears. Good scenarios are emotional because they draw upon the range of human emotions to make their case. It is in this way that we can become engaged with the futures represented within the scenarios – we want to own them or disown them, depending upon whether we find them appealing or unappealing.

Normally a futures project is not open ended. We normally have a focus and we normally have a time horizon to provide a boundary. The focus of a futures project could be very wide, such as the future of a given nation or organisation, or it could be very narrow, such as the future of something quite specific, like retailing. The key difference between the two types of futures with which we are concerned is the number of key variables that will impact upon that future. Generally speaking, if the focus of a futures project is very broad, it will have a larger number of key variables that will impact upon it. As the one increases, so does the other.

This has a direct bearing upon the complexity of the futures that we are describing. If the scenarios contain a large number of uncertain factors that interact with each other in complex and uncertain ways, then it is obvious that the resulting scenarios will be quite involved and, when viewed through the lens of a predictive forecast, will contain a large margin of error. We can reasonably say that there is a direct link between the focus of a project, the number of factors involved in viewing the future, and the uncertainty and complexity of the possible outcomes within that future. A broader focus will contain a larger set of elements, which will interact to produce a more uncertain range of possible future outcomes.

A similar situation applies to the time horizon of the project. It is normally the case that the longer the project looks into the future; the greater will be the uncertainty about how specific the scenarios can be. We can be more certain about the course of a shorter time horizon than we can be about a longer time horizon. This is because the critical uncertainties to our future vision will have longer to play out in a longer time horizon. Over a longer time horizon, factors of which we currently are unaware of – the 'unknown unknowns', as some call them - will have time to develop and possibly dominate the future that we are describing.

It is for this reason that we need to be specific about the assumptions that we are to include in our future visions. It is unlikely that we shall be able to capture fully all of the factors that may impact upon our future vision. There are some factors that we shall have to deem as relatively unimportant, and which can reasonably be set aside. Whilst there will also be other factors that we judge to be of critical importance, and which will be quite central to our future scenarios. It may turn out that we are wrong in our judgement, and that the discarded factors become more important than the factors that we previously deemed to be critical in our vision of the future. In this case, we need the ability to flex our scenarios to accommodate this new future as it evolves.

It is often said that one of the roles of a futures project is to answer one or more questions about the future, and that the secret to finding good answers to the question is to have a good question to begin with. This is normally found in the terms of reference of the project. The terms of reference ought to highlight what it is that the project is looking at – which, by definition, also determines what the project is not looking at – and the time horizon with which the project is concerned. It is only when the objective has been established that we can begin to define what assumptions to bring to the project, and what to discount. Of these assumptions, some will be critical to the formation of the future visions, whilst others will play a lesser role.

This was the process that we used in developing our 'Communities Of The Future' project. The project arose in 2010 from the concerns of a number of people in the English county of Suffolk about how local public services could withstand the impact of a prolonged period of fiscal austerity. With many regards, the anticipated baseline future was one of much increased demands for public services whilst, at the same time, the resource base from which those services were to be financed would be ever shrinking. A phrase much used at the time was that service delivery needed to be much smarter in its focus, and that foresight could help in the process of making it smarter.

The first main question that faced the project was the time horizon to which it addressed. We opted for 2030 as a target date because it served a number of needs. It provided us with an horizon that was outside of the normal planning horizon, but not so far in the future to be beyond the reckoning of policy-makers. The bulk of the work was conducted between 2010 and 2012, which meant that the horizon of 2030 was about a generation away. From an emotional perspective, it is easier to talk of the future legacy that we are handing our children. It is also a point in time where, although there is a strong echo from the present, there is also a different feel to it.

When we considered the question of how that different feel would manifest itself, we came up with two answers. First, it was held that climate change would be felt more acutely in 2030 when compared to 2010. This would manifest itself in a more extreme range of temperatures (much hotter summers and more cold winters), more erratic weather patterns (more storms and longer dry spells), a changing pattern to the weather (the seasons becoming a bit more jumbled). We can point to current evidence of this, and decided to exaggerate the trend, not to more extremes, but just to make it more pronounced.

The second difference we thought to be more pronounced in 2030 would be the impact of resource scarcity. Looking initially at energy and fuel, and building out to include many other commodities, we took as a background assumption that the impact of more scarce resources would be more evident in 2030 when compared to 2010. We took the view that this would manifest itself in the higher price of these resources for the end consumer, and that social structures would be stressed as a result. It is easy for this background assumption to form the basis of a dystopian view of the future. We were at pains to avoid that view by highlighting the opportunities that a period of resource scarcity could generate, and that we could quite well build a number of utopian scenarios around this.

It could be argued that these assumptions are likely to be incorrect. Some might argue that the impact of climate change by 2030 has been much exaggerated whilst others might argue that any incipient resource scarcities are likely to have resolved themselves by 2030. Both positions can be argued well, but, for the purposes of this project, we wanted to see what would happen if both of these assumptions proved to be correct. Could we find a positive future in the face of resource scarcity? Can we learn to live with the effects of disruptive climate change? We saw these questions as more interesting, so we retained them as core assumptions.

We also had to give some thought to the focus of the project. As stated earlier, the project originated in the English county of Suffolk. Suffolk is a small, rural, county that is located about seventy miles away from London. One of the critical uncertainties that Suffolk faces in the years to 2030 is the link to London, both by road and by rail. At present, the road and rail links are considered to be inadequate for the present needs. There is a political desire to improve the road and rail links to London. Some of our scenarios assume that the links are improved, with both positive and negative impacts. This issue will be encountered in both out utopian and dystopian scenarios.

One of the concerns about Suffolk is that a relatively large part of the current level of economic activity within the county is derived from the agricultural base. Traditionally, jobs in this sector tend to be low value added, which means that incomes in Suffolk are below the national average. There is a concern, at the policy level, about how to raise the general levels of income within the county.

One way to do this would be to encourage the level of entrepreneurial activity within the county, which defined one of the communities with which we are concerned – The Entrepreneurial Community. The utopian scenario outlines some of the key elements of what we feel that a successful small business would contain in 2030, whilst the dystopian scenario explores what is likely to hold business back. Both scenarios assume improved rail links to London.

Upon consideration of The Entrepreneurial Community, it was found that there is a prior requisite, which is the existence of a hub of creativity. Suffolk currently lacks that hub at any meaningful level. This defined our second community with which we are concerned – The Creative Community.

Our focus here was to consider what a successful Creative Community would look like in our utopian scenario, and what the barriers to the establishment of that community would be in our dystopian scenario.

Like most English counties, Suffolk has an ageing population, which is likely to become more prominent in the years to 2030. There is a policy concern about how public services can be maintained and improved as demand grows and the expected resource base to meet that demand diminishes. This concern gave rise to the third community with which we are concerned – The Caring Community. As we stated earlier, it was held that the key to adapting to this operational environment would be working smarter rather than harder. Our utopian scenario explores what a smarter operational environment might look like, whilst the dystopian scenario considers what life would be like if we are unable to work smarter. In many respects, the dystopian scenario represents a projection of current trends out to 2030.

A feature of Suffolk is that it has a coastline that is designated an 'Area Of Outstanding Natural Beauty'. This gives rise to a number of conflicting interests between the various stakeholders. Our fourth community – The Coastal Community – consists of a number of these stakeholders. If, as we have assumed, disruptive climate change starts to be felt by 2030, then how will the balance of these conflicting interests be affected? Our utopian scenario considers how these changes might be beneficial, whilst our dystopian scenario reminds us that change does not always come without some cost. Together, both scenarios embrace change and looks to see how it might impact upon Suffolk.

Our final community – The Food Community - returns to the agricultural base in Suffolk. Farming is so dominant in Suffolk that it is not possible to exclude it as a feature of life in 2030. The utopian scenario starts with a personal tragedy and expands out to find a good outcome in the face of disruptive climate change and resource scarcity. The dystopian scenario explores some of the consequences of disruptive climate change as it impacts upon agriculture in 2030. In many respects, the difference between the two scenarios is that, in the utopian scenario change is used positively, whereas in the dystopian scenario change is resisted with some unfortunate consequences.

This point addresses the purpose of this book. We have included a utopian scenario and a dystopian scenario for each of the communities because we want the utopian scenarios to inspire the reader to develop their own preferred future, to want to go out and build that future. We want the dystopian scenario to act as a warning to the reader about how we can sleepwalk into a future that we might want to avoid; we want to encourage them to act now to avoid that future. It is underwritten by our belief that we can create our own future.

The book begins with the Creative Community, followed by the Entrepreneurial Community. The two chapters should be seen as a pair that ought to be read together. We then move on to the Caring Community to remind us that community is about more than just the acquisition of wealth. From there we consider the Coastal Community, which, in addition to being tied to a specific location in Suffolk, also acts as an extension of the Caring Community. Finally, we review the Food Community, which brings together some of the themes considered in the previous four communities, and which also provides a backdrop of rural Suffolk.

In the development of the scenarios, we have produced a character set which the reader bumps into a number of times. In many ways this reflects the nature of life in Suffolk. It is one of the more sparsely populated counties in England, and there is more than an element of truth to the view that a lot of people know each other. We thought that this would give a good feel for the scenarios, along with providing a thread that underlines the fact that one person can simultaneously belong to a number of communities.

What will Suffolk look like in 2030? In one respect, we haven't a clue. In another respect, we are now starting to define how we want it to look. By creating a vision of Suffolk in 2030 and inviting people to help us build that vision – or, if necessary, help us to amend that vision – the county will be as we are currently creating it. It is said that we get the future we deserve. Let us hope that our desserts contain more of the positive visions laid out in this book and fewer of the negative ones. The future belongs to us all, so it is up to us to ensure that we have a good one.

CHAPTER 2

THE CREATIVE COMMUNITY

For those areas that want to thrive in the modern world, it is seen as imperative to foster a creative community. Suffolk is no exception here. An important part of thriving is to have a prosperous community, one that also has a great deal of social cohesion. A creative community is central to achieving that ambition. One feature of the modern world is how information technology has completely changed the way in which organisations operate. The commercial premium is now upon the use of knowledge, and we have seen the rise of the Knowledge Economy.

A key aspect of the Knowledge Economy is the role that the creative community plays within it. In terms of process, the creative community generates material that adds to what we already know – our stock of creative capital. This gives rise to a process of creative capital accumulation, which is used to generate commercial opportunities. As these opportunities are taken, a process occurs where further prosperity is generated. And so the cycle goes on as rising prosperity creates further knowledge generation.

This process is greatly enhanced if the creative agents – the individual members of the creative community – live in close proximity to one another. This close proximity, whether physical or virtual, allows the various creative agents to interact with each other to generate new ideas. The realisation of which becomes the creative capital. Whilst virtual proximity does have a positive effect, the process of idea creation is even more effective if there is a form of physical proximity for the creative agents.

This begs the question: what factors are likely to lead creative agents to live in a given place? There is no single factor that stands out as particularly dominant, but a range of factors do contribute to the decision about where to live. Diversity is an important factor that allows for the cross-fertilisation of ideas. If there is uniformity to the community, then established ideas are unlikely to be challenged and novelty is unlikely to be found. In order to enhance this diversity, the community needs to be reasonably tolerant of a multiplicity of ideas. This tolerance needs to extend to a tolerance of diverse lifestyles as well as diverse opinions, as people generally incline to live their lives according to their beliefs. Finally, the community needs to be open and welcoming to newcomers. This openness is an expression of the tolerance within the community and will result in a diverse community.

The process of developing a creative community could be assisted by a number of relatively simple policy initiatives. Policy makers could focus upon making an area a great place to live. This means providing the appropriate arts, cultural, and recreational facilities that creative agents demand. Assistance could be given to developing a forum that acts as a local bootstrap for the creation of intellectual property – a source of technology, talent, and social tolerance. In this way, a 'people climate' rather than a 'business climate' could be developed to attract the creative agents to an area.

It has to be remembered that creative agents, whilst attracted to diverse, tolerant, and open communities, are also repelled by communities that lack a vision of the future, which are trapped in the past, and whose vested interests generate a resistance to change. This is one of the reasons why Suffolk does not have a creative community. There is no vision of the future that inspires people to want to build it. As a community, Suffolk is trapped by its heritage, which means that, as a community, it tends to be a laggard to novelty rather than an early adopter. In part, this is because the vested interests are so dominant that change is slow and patchy. Their lack of foresight means that Suffolk reacts to the future rather than leads it.

It doesn't have to be that way, and this is the starting point for our scenarios. In many respects, the dystopian scenario was easier to write. This is simply a case of taking the current trajectory for Suffolk and extending it out to 2030. It is a world with very little foresight, where new ideas are not encouraged, where small business continues to be in the grip of large corporate financial institutions, and where agribusiness is still dominant in the rural community. Creativity does not flourish in an environment where it is not encouraged.

The utopian scenario was much harder to produce because it involves thinking about a world that has never existed in Suffolk. In developing the scenario, we thought it important to place it in a creative enterprise hub. These have been tried before in Suffolk, but to no great success. What is different about the hub in our scenario is its mission. We see it as acting as part of a wider community, the purpose of which is not just delivering financial prosperity, but also helping to establish a form of community cohesion. We could almost style it as generating social capital as well as monetary capital. It is this social capital that allows the hub to act as a bootstrap for generating creative capital.

This feeds into another agenda that we see as worth exploring out to 2030 – the extent to which we will return to 'business as usual' corporatism as we move from recession to recovery. The establishment of creative hubs is one way to reject the pursuit of money whilst embracing the need to earn a living. For this reason, it represents an extension of a trend that may come to dominate the commercial world in the coming decades. It is almost as if this would provide a way for business to reconnect to the society again, which brings us full circle to our original point. For there to be a prosperous community, there needs to be a high degree of social cohesion. The creative community is the vehicle through which this could be achieved in the future, which is why it is an important community to consider.

West Suffolk Creative Ltd (WSC)

A company limited by guarantee.

Tenth Annual General Meeting held at Cafe Vision, The Innovation Centre, Mildenhall on 31 October 2030

Board Members

Kai Radar, Director, A Journey In Time, (WSC Chair)

Red Thornton, Director, Future Studies Unit

Calise Roadnight, Director, Forward Vision

Ben Salmon, Creative Director, Techno Jam

Sammy Lee Huggins, Proprietor, Cafe Vision

Amelia Kim, Chief Executive, Pendlebury Associates (Also WSC Treasurer)

Tempest Heath, Director, Creative Holograms

Jet Hunsden, Director, Meta Materials

Victoria Chalk, Director, Rejuvenation

Zac Newland, Director, Suffolk Bioinformatic Solutions (SBS)

Robert Newman, Director, Newman Enterprises

Jed Harris, Director, AFS Ltd (Alternative Farming Solutions)

Approval of the previous minutes held on 28 September 2029

The Minutes of the AGM held on 28 September 2029 were duly approved.

Matters Arising from the last AGM

1. Masters Programme in Future Studies

Red Thornton, Director of Future Studies at The Mildenhall Centre of Learning Excellence, reported that the Masters programme had now been set up with funding from the WSC accumulated fund. The degree had been approved as an external degree by the University of

Cambridge, taught and delivered in Mildenhall[1]. Twenty post-graduate students from across the world were now enrolled. Classes had just started and students were currently being allocated to their relevant workplace internships[2]. Red informed the meeting that he had started to work with the European Futures Observatory, based in Ipswich, to encourage renowned futurists from other parts of the world to deliver parts of the programme. It was hoped that some of the students would be able to attend the AGM next year to report on their experiences.

2. Community Enterprise Scheme

Following the announcement at last year's AGM of the £3.2 million legacy bequeathed by founding member Jodie Cushion, it was decided by the members to initiate a Community Enterprise Scheme that would help to strengthen civil society in West Suffolk[3]. Each year, WSC would add to the endowment of the scheme through a distribution from the accumulated fund. It was agreed that Calise Roadnight and Ben Salmon would report back with the progress to date.

Calise reported that the following framework had been adopted:
- **Project based grants** providing financial assistance for community organisations, for the purchase of equipment, construction or renovation of premises and funding for specific unforeseen events,

---

[1] We take the view that, by 2030, much of teaching in higher education will be fairly distributed compared to today. The learning will go to the students rather than having the students go to the learning. The advance of communication technologies will enable this development.

[2] We anticipate a much closer relationship between business and the academic community if both are to thrive. We have assumed severe limitations on the public funding of higher education, which has the potential to change the nature of the way in which higher education is funded.

[3] We have assumed that predatory capitalism no longer appears to be a viable option for small business. We see the small business community as the more effective agency of change within the business community, and a readiness to invest in community activities as the public sector withdraws from them.

such as disaster management projects[4]. To date, £0.4 million had been allocated to projects.

- **Community Operating Grants** providing financial assistance to non-profit organizations in West Suffolk to enhance the organisation's ability to operate and deliver services to the community[5]. To date, £1.2 million had been allocated to projects.

- **International Development Grants** to continue Jodie's vision to help build sustainable communities in the emerging world by providing financial assistance to Suffolk based NGOs to give people in developing countries the tools needed to provide a sustainable environment in which to work. To date, £1.3 million had been allocated to projects.

Treasurers Report

1. As Treasurer of WSC, Amelia Kim presented to the meeting the accounts for the year to 30th June 2030.

2. Amelia reported that the company had enjoyed another very good year. Income from the profit sharing and loan arrangements with member companies had increased by 37%, taking turnover to £9.8 million for the year. Operating costs had been held to £1 million, which meant that, after corporation tax, just over £7 million would be posted to the accumulated fund[6].

---

[4] We have assumed that the incidence of climate originated disruptions, such as violent storms and flooding, will be more prevalent in the years to 2030. At the same time, owing to budgetary constraints, the ability of public agencies to respond to those events will diminish. Our assumption is that the financial gap between need and delivery will be met by public philanthropy, mainly from the small business sector.

[5] Business benefits from many of the public services, such as education and housing, which are provided at the local level. In the years to 2030, as the levels of public provision of those services falls compared to today, we have assumed that the small business sector will step in to fund that shortfall.

[6] We have assumed a funding structure for the company whereby the users of the technology hub pay a form of revenue sharing and profit sharing for their membership. The hub takes an equity stake in each resident, becoming a hybrid form of venture fund. We

3. In accordance with the decisions of previous years, it was proposed that £1 million would be allocated to fund the Masters Programme in Futures Studies and to provide financial assistance to students joining the programme, £2 million would be provided to the Community Enterprise Scheme, £2 million would be donated to local community initiatives as a Social Dividend, and that the balance should be retained for future projects.

4. The proposal to allocate the 2029-30 surplus was unanimously agreed by all members present, and the accounts for the year were accordingly adopted.

5. As Chair of the company, Kai thanked Amelia for all of her hard work over the past year as Treasurer.

Members Reports

1. A Journey In Time – Kai reported to the meeting that his business continued to prosper, and that the move from being a consultancy based organisation to being one that had future commercial opportunities as its focus had accelerated over the past year. The balance of clients continued to move away from Europe and North America towards Asia, and was expected to do so for some time to come[7]. Kai stated that he was looking to make a better use of communications technology – especially holographic technologies[8] – to reduce the amount of travelling that he

---

have assumed that the banking sector continues to serve small business badly, and for this reason the hub advances loans to members to help fund their expansion and growth.

[7] We have assumed that the growth generator in the global economy will continue to be Asia, and that the key to the successful development of small business in Suffolk would be the ability to take advantage of that growth. Developments in communications technology will continue to enhance this trend.

[8] We have assumed that, by 2030, the use of holographic communications technology will be sufficiently common for it not to be out of the ordinary. This has the potential to enhance the reach of the service sector, who are even less likely to be tied to a physical location.

had to undertake. There was the possibility of opening an office in Singapore, which he expected to do in the coming year.

2. Cafe Vision – Sammy Lee reported that the cafe had expanded its opening hours to 24 hours a day and had developed themed lounges. Night sessions were proving popular with insomniacs who chilled out on beanbags in the Jamming Lounge while listening to live music and thrashing out ideas. Demand from musicians was high with the cafe attracting itinerant groups from all over the world, especially after the band Flying Colours was catapulted to fame after being spotted on the webcam by a recording studio in Los Angeles. In the Fun Factory, day time crèche facilities[9] have been extended to include a play scheme during the school holidays while the Break Out Zone is still a popular rendezvous for meetings, connecting with clients or just having a coffee with friends. The meeting was amused to learn that despite the cafe's high spec communications network, the most popular tools were still the white and black boards.

3. Pendlebury Associates – Although based in Bury St Edmunds Amelia has had an association with WSC for some years. She reported that 2010 had been a busy year for the company's avatar management services and had been awarded its biggest contract to date from a company who needed to wipe clean unfavourable information on a number of their key directors. Due to Amelia being heavily pregnant she left the meeting early as she was feeling unwell. Everyone wished her the best with the imminent birth of her twins.

4. Creative Holograms – Tempest reported that since 2012 when the government lifted restrictions on the controversial practice of fracking, the business had continued to grow. By developing models using 'hard'

[9] We have assumed that a positive future would be one in which business develops to make its practices child friendly. We see it essential for business to offer those working in business the opportunity for a full family life, and locally based crèches, funded by business are a way forward in this area.

21

holograms to determine the viability and compatibility of the fracking industry, the company had become a world leader in providing accurate data for underground exploration[10]. The main impetus for this has come from the insistence of insurance companies that a complex analysis be made to forecast likely hot spots for seismic movements and volcanic eruptions. It has also proved instrumental in the successful rescue of personnel from collapsed mines in Africa and South America.

5. Techno Jam – Ben Salmon reported that following on from the success of the annual WSIF (West Suffolk Ideas Festival) over the last three years, his company had acquired a redundant RAF aircraft hanger and was in the process of converting this into film and recording studios[11]. This would be up and running for next year's conference in August 2031 to complement the trade show which had proved successful in attracting organisations instrumental in building relationships between media, technology, their creators and the consumers. There would also be space to hold an 'Emergence Hub' to encourage future entrepreneurs to benefit from networking with investors from every sector of the creative industry. Ben reminded the meeting that without help from a similar scheme in Austin, Texas, he would never had got his business off the ground and been able to relocate back to Suffolk with his family after spending twenty years in California.

6. Meta Materials – now in its fifteenth year, Jet reported that the company had been awarded a contract with British Aeronautics for its work on stealth technology with the development of its patented 'meta materials'. After a decade of research the company had a breakthrough

---

[10] We have assumed that commercial activities are not without external constraints. We have assumed a link between the practice of hydraulic fracturing (fracking) and seismic activity, which has led regulators to require full three dimensional modelling of any proposed operations as a precautionary measure.

[11] We have assumed a closer relationship between the arts and cultural sectors and the business sector. The relationship is more than financial. The generation of new ideas is central to the creative community, which leads to a greater willingness of the business community to support the creative sector.

in 2019 and had finally discovered the formula to successfully cloak objects. The size of the object being cloaked had increased dramatically over the past decade, with the major impetus coming from the defence and security sector. The company had a number of forward contracts that Jet was unable to share with the meeting, owing to their sensitive nature[12].

7. Rejuvenation – Victoria reported that the company continues to develop its research links with Cornell and Cambridge Universities into developing one-stop shops to print and replace body parts[13]. Victoria modelled her new right ear which had been replaced following a car accident last year. New franchises are opening in London, Paris and New York to with the fashion industry showing a particular interest. Victoria hoped that the company would be able to expand its core technology into the Asian market in the next five years.

8. Forward Vision – Calise reported that the company was working with Moorfield Eye Hospital to roll out a programme of retinal implant facilities and now had 20 centres around the country. In addition, with the help of an International Development Grant from The Community Enterprise Scheme, Calise stated that it is the aim of the company to trial a mobile unit in West Africa and, if successful, train a local medical team to establish this on a more permanent basis. Ultimately, the intention is to spread this technique globally[14].

---

[12] An important land use in Suffolk is for military bases. We have assumed a close link between Suffolk businesses and the military, particularly in the area of developing the early stages of future technologies.

[13] We have assumed that the development of 3D printing techniques has developed sufficiently to allow for the printing of replacement body parts by 2030. At first a development in the field of medicine, our story assumes that, by 2030, such enhancements for cosmetic reasons will start to come to market. We have also assumed a roll out in Europe and North America at first, followed by maturation in Asia.

[14] We anticipate this technology to restore sight to those who have lost it. We have also included a dimension to remind us that this issue not only affects us in Suffolk, but has an impact across the globe. We have used this as an example of how socially minded businesses can use their developments to benefit more than just their core constituency.

9. Suffolk Bioinformatic Solutions – Zac reported that demand for bioinformatics databases were growing with interest ranging from the IT, pharmaceutical and banking sectors. With the current shortage of raw materials, industry is taking a keen interest in the company's landfill mapping database that was developed as an off-shoot from a previous project[15]. The company is continuing to work alongside The Sanger Institute, a leader in the human genome project, to obtain a better understanding how genetics can be used in disease prevention, and the European Bioinformatics Institute, both based in Cambridge.

10. Newman Enterprises – Robert reported that the operating facility had now totally relocated to Suffolk after continuous cost overruns in the manufacturing facility in China. The set up grant from the Suffolk Ventures Board had helped to defray some of the cost of establishing a new manufacturing unit in Haverhill and the first run of suitcases came off the production line in April in time to reach the summer vacation market[16]. Robert thanked other members of WSC for their help and support, and reported his intention – with the help of other WSC members - to use 3D printing in the production of the next generation of smart suitcases.

11. Alternative Farming Solutions – Having worked in farming all his life, Jedd Harris set up AFS last year in response to the dire state of affairs of farming in East Anglia. Being the first recipient of a grant from the Community Enterprise Scheme, he reported that he has acquired some land and has been reaching out to the local farming community to

---

[15] We have assumed that, by 2030, the scarcity of key resources is such that it is commercially viable to mount a salvage operation from parcels of land that were formerly used as landfill. In the past, resources capable of salvage were simply discarded, and we anticipate that there will come a time when we will mine the past rubbish dumps for materials that still have value.

[16] Whilst we see the continued economic development of Asia, we have also assumed that it will no longer be the low cost manufacturing hub for Europe and North America. We envisage that the rising cost of transportation, along with the falling cost of manufacturing at home, will lead to a number of small manufacturers bringing production back to the UK.

try and overcome the ever increasing obstacles put in the path of the arable farmer. Jedd stated that it had become obvious that if something was not done to improve crop yields, the downward trend in arable harvests due to adverse weather conditions would only set to continue. With farmers having to keep their livestock indoors during the summer period because of flooding, something had to be done. The company is in the early stages of development but Jedd is in the process of setting up co-operative scheme where farmers can pool their resources and expertise, which he hopes to extend by including students from Brandon Academy[17].

Closing Presentation

To close the meeting a presentation was made by students from Brandon Academy, the local high school, highlighting the work they have undertaken with Alternative Farming Solutions in developing renewable energy sources. By utilising waste from local farms they plan to convert waste into biogas which the farmers can then use on their machinery. The Academy acts as a beacon school of good practice in preparing young people for the world of work by working closely with the businesses located at WSC[18]. It is planned to show how this is working in schools and colleges across Suffolk and Cambridgeshire.

Date of Next Meeting – Saturday, 27 September 2031

It was agreed that Techno Space will host next year's AGM in the afternoon to be followed by a concert and party in The Hangar.

---

[17] It tends to be forgotten that farming is an important part of commercial activity in Suffolk. We have assumed that farming becomes more difficult in the years to 2030 owing to the rising cost of key, oil-based, agricultural inputs; along with falling crop yields resulting from climate change. We wanted to include a school in the story, just to remind us that farming is an activity undertaken by the whole community.

[18] We have assumed that there is a greater integration of the business and education sectors by 2030. Schools are more responsive to the needs of local businesses, and local businesses come to recognise that they have an interest in creating a business literate workforce.

Banking On A Change

The squalling shriek of the seagull caught James' attention as he climbed the steps of the bank, its sound transporting him back to a happier time. A small white feather drifted down in front of his face and, looking up, he discovered a line of seagulls standing sentinel on the tiled roof above him. James shivered. It felt as though they were passing judgement.

"Welcome to The Global Banking Centre[19]. How can I be of help today?"

James stood in front of the projected hologram[20].

"I have an appointment to see a personal advisor. My name's James Godbold."

The image flickered momentarily as a pale blue light washed over him, the barrier parted[21].

"Your appointment with Mr Cheeseman is scheduled for 11:00 o'clock. Please take a seat. While you are waiting let me direct you to The Fair

---

[19] We have assumed the continued operation of a globally oriented banking sector, which has little locally based competition. In this framework, our assumptions include one that peer-to-peer lending does not achieve critical mass to be widely experienced.

[20] Our assumption is that the customer experience of the banking sector continues to be impersonal. However, by 2030, we do envisage that smart holograms will have replaced call centres at the first point of contact for the customer.

[21] Access to banking halls is an important part of the experience of banking for many customers. We see a greater divide between those who may enter the banking hall, and those who are to be kept out. Ostensibly for security purposes, we see these as exacerbating current levels of inequality.

Exchange[22] coffee lounge at the rear of the banking hall where our market day special includes a croissant with a freshly ground cup of Java coffee. A bargain at only £20.00."

James stepped through the barrier and walked towards a crescent of low backed leatherette sofas. The smell of freshly brewed coffee made his stomach rumble, but coffee would have to be put on hold, he must stay focussed. The bank looked busy but James spotted a seat in the waiting area between a mother trying to stop her screaming toddler from running off and a hooded teenager slouched over two seats at the end of the row. Guess I'm not the only one down on my luck, James thought as he sat down beside the teenager who grunted as he shuffled along the seat, never taking his eyes from the screen on his wrist[23]. James felt a sinking feeling forming in the pit of his stomach. Already his suit was uncomfortable and the crowded journey on the bus this morning had not put him in a good frame of mind.

It had not always been like this. Born at the start of the new millennium, James had lived what many would call a charmed life. Now his financial situation was so dire he could not even afford to get his car repaired. The final humiliation was that he had to use public transport. The twice weekly bus service into Bury St Edmunds was at best inadequate and at worst unreliable[24].

---

[22] It is our view that banks, whilst continuing to be de-humanised and impersonal, will also attempt to engage in forms of social responsibility, but on a commercial scale. We question the effectiveness of such schemes.

[23] We have assumed that teenagers are very little different in 2030 as they are today. The gadgets that they have access to will change. We have included an example of wrist borne personalised technology to express our view that gadgets will change, but not by a great margin.

[24] One of the issues currently facing rural communities is public transport. The current situation is that it tends to be patchy in coverage. We have assumed that this continues to be the case, and that the situation will worsen in the years to 2030. We want to include an assumption of unreliability to public transport in this world, where the scheduled services are rarely delivered.

"Mr Gadbolt?" announced a callow faced youth as he peered down into a small hand held monitor[25].

James stood up and followed the bank clerk into glass fronted meeting room.

"My name is Cheeseman and I'm your personal advisor today. Do take a seat."

"Actually," James said, "my name is Godbold, James Godbold, Josh to my friends."

Cheeseman ran a hand through his greasy brown hair and smiled.

"Godbold. I do apologise. Now let me bring up your details."

After several taps on the small black monitor in his hand, James' bank details were projected onto the metallic desk in front of him[26]. Cheeseman screwed up his eyes and turned to James.

"What can I do for you today?"

The scene James had rehearsed in his head evaporated. The bank clerk looked no older than his kid brother at university, how could he possibly understand the complexities of running a business?

"I need a loan," James blurted out.

---

[25] To emphasise the impersonal nature of the banking offering, we wanted to highlight that a greater reliance upon technology does not necessarily mean an improvement in service levels. Despite having access to banks of information, the clerk is unable to get the customer's name right.

[26] We have assumed a greater use of light and information projection in our scenario. Rather than having physical screens, the data contained in the system is projected onto a surface for access.

A few more taps on the monitor and the figures on the screen changed to red.

"I see that you were based at Bridge Farm. Our records say this has recently been repossessed."

The past year had possibly been the worst one of James's life. The farm had been in his family for generations and for James it had provided a base from which to build up a business community based on creativity and knowledge[27].

"Yeah, the farm was taken away from us," James said. "It was the second mortgage which landed the farm in trouble, that and the soaring cost of diesel which meant there just wasn't the cash flow to run the machinery. Even when Dad tried to sell some of it off, he got rock bottom prices as the market was flooded with out of date technology.[28]" Cheeseman nodded sympathetically.

"On top of that was the erratic rainfall. With drought in spring and deluges of rain in summer, it became impossible to know when to sow and when to harvest. Seeds designed to withstand drought could not cope with the flooding whilst seeds adapted for wet weather could not cope with the long dry spells. As a result yields declined and the farm fell behind on its interest payments and Global called in their loan. It was at this point Dad realised he would lose the farm his great, great grandfather had started[29].

---

[27] The dystopian scenario is meant to provide a counterpoint to the utopian one. In this scenario, a creative hub was formed, but has failed. Our point is that success cannot be guaranteed in such ventures. To be successful, they have to be nurtured and encouraged.

[28] An important point here is that when technology advances rapidly, the built in period of obsolescence for the machinery shortens. We have combined a series of poor harvests, over extended bank borrowing, and shortened obsolescence as the trigger that makes the farm unviable.

[29] We have included this point to highlight the distance between a globally based organisation and the local communities in which they operate. In this case, tradition and history count for nothing when the numbers run against the local business. Rather than assisting the farm to turn around, it is easier for the bank to put it into liquidation.

The final blow for Dad was when he was diagnosed with lung cancer, after that the fight went out of him."

"I can sympathise with your father's predicament," Cheeseman said, "but what has that got to do with your application for a loan today?"

James pulled a notebook out of his top pocket, keyed in his pass code and watched the screen come to life.

"Everything," James said as he projected a three dimensional hologram onto the desk in front of the bank clerk. "Ten years ago I converted a barn into a business centre combining offices with a base for a library, shop and a community cafe. Some great ideas came out of there, look I can show you some of them." James worked his way through the files to illustrate them.

"All very interesting," Cheeseman cut in, "but how can the bank help you today?"

"When fuel prices rose to over £15.00 a litre some of the businesses decided to relocate to Ipswich and Bury where there were good transport links. Plus at that time our broadband coverage was patchy[30]. The final nail in the coffin was losing the farm. Look, this will show you what happened to my business," James said changing the image from a converted barn to a massive storage facility.

"When the bank took over the farm and sold it off I lost my business as well. The barns and offices were demolished and five huge silos put up in their place. I tried to negotiate with the new owners to lease our farm house so that Dad would not have to move, but that was sold to a City Financier as

---

[30] We have assumed that good public transport and communications links are a precondition for the development of rural communities. They are currently inadequate, and we have assumed that position worsens in the years to 2030.

a weekend retreat. He was attracted to the area by improved rail links, as you know the journey time to Liverpool Street is now only 50 minutes[31].

"The new owners of the farm, a syndicate based in Hong Kong, were not interested in local initiatives. The only thing which motivated them was buying up land. In fact they've bought out three farms in the area already. It was heartbreaking to see the soul taken out of the community and it's my aim to put it back. What I need from Global Bank is a mortgage to secure the old village Post Office which has recently come on the market, and some working capital to get the operation up and running.[32]"

Cheeseman rubbed his chin with his hand. "I see, and do you have a business plan to support this?"

Flicking through the screens on his monitor James located the figures he was after and projected them on to the table for Cheeseman to view. James knew this was his weak spot. In the past he would have engaged an accountant but with his finances the way they were, he could not afford accountant's fees. He had put together the figures himself.

James sat back in his seat to give Cheeseman space to study his figures. Each time he tapped the screen James noticed a slight twitch in his right eye, and after what seemed like an age Cheeseman looked up.

"I'm afraid, Mr Godbold, your figures do not meet the criteria required by Global Bank to extend credit to you today. An email will follow explaining this in more detail. However, if you would like to re-assess your projections do feel free to schedule another appointment when we would be happy to

---

[31] We have assumed that land continues to have a use. The agricultural land is used to parcel into ever larger units for prairie style farming, whilst the farm buildings have a residential use, mainly for wealthy Londoners. In this scenario, Suffolk becomes more like a Home Counties dormitory.

[32] It is at this point that the contrast between global finance and local communities comes into focus. We had the syndicate based in Hong Kong because, by 2030, we see Europe becoming an investment destination for the new wealthy in Asia.

speak to you further. We value your custom. Your success is our success.[33]"

James turned off his notebook and slid it back into his pocket. Taking Cheeseman's proffered hand, he stood up and left. God, he must think I'm a right fool, James thought as he made his way to the entrance barrier, can't even convince a schoolboy that I've a viable business plan.

The lingering smell of coffee reminded him that he had not had any breakfast, but there was no way he would get it here, James wanted to get out of this place as quickly as possible.

"I'm sorry we were unable to help you today," said the hologram who had greeted James on his way in, "Global Bank looks forward to serving you again soon."

James passed through the open sliding door and pulled out his notebook to check the time, he would have to hurry if he was to get everything done before he caught the bus home. Standing for a moment to let the crisp autumn air revive him, he puzzled over his predicament; it seemed no matter how hard he tried, there was never enough money. Oh well, James thought, can't hang around here, I'd best make a move. Walking through the line of market stalls[34] James noticed an illuminated hoarding proclaiming *"Local Businesswoman nominated as Entrepreneur of the Year"*. As he walked closer he saw the name flash across the screen, Amelia Kim.

"I'll be damned; Milly has hit the big time!" James exclaimed.

---

[33] We have assumed the continued use of computer based credit scoring to determine whether or not a loan would be advanced. On the one hand, the decision is delivered rather coldly and impersonally, whilst, on the other, there is a veneer of customer care. This is the experience of many of the banking sector today, and we have assumed that it does not improve by 2030.

[34] Irrespective of how high tech the local economy becomes, we have assumed that traditional forms of shopping, such a local markets, will continue.

Keying the speed dial on his notebook James waited to be connected to Amelia's phone, instead a message flashed up saying he was out of credit. He flicked the screen off and shoved the notepad into his pocket muttering under his breath.

"It's the first sign of madness you know," James turned to find his girlfriend, Milly, clutching a huge shopping bag, "talking to yourself." Never had he needed a friendly face more than now. "I've had a pig of a morning," James said. "Fancy buying me a coffee?"

CHAPTER 3

THE ENTREPRENEURIAL COMMUNITY

Our concern for the entrepreneurial community is based upon the belief that it is the source of future prosperity and employment growth. It is generally stated that small to medium sized enterprises (SMEs) are the place in which entrepreneurship resides. This creates a model where, in order to obtain prosperity and employment growth, we need to encourage entrepreneurship, and that can be achieved by encouraging SMEs.

It is possible to dispute this view if many of the SMEs that are created are lifestyle businesses where there is little aspiration for growth beyond providing a comfortable lifestyle for the owners of the SMEs. We wanted our scenarios to embrace this duality. In the utopian scenario (Lucky Stars) the business owner had a great drive to create a business empire, the centre of which would be at Bury St Edmunds. In the dystopian scenario (Life's Not Fare – A Taxi Driver's Tale) the business owner aspires little in life beyond getting by.

In many respects, this defines the purpose of this pair of scenarios. If our aim is to ensure that Suffolk has a prosperous future, then we need to inspire entrepreneurs who want to create a business empire from a base in Suffolk. Policy initiatives can assist this process, but without the people to drive it forward it will not happen. That is the crucial link between the creative community and the entrepreneurial community. For prosperity to occur there has to be the commercial exploitation of creative ideas. A successful outcome needs to blend the creative with the entrepreneurial.

There are four key stages to the development of an SME. We like to state them in terms of the natural world because this gives a sense of growing a successful SME. To start with, there are the Seeds – SMEs that are at the pre-revenue stage, where costs are incurred, but at which there is no corresponding revenue. Beyond that are the Seedlings – SMEs that have started to generate revenue, but for which costs still dominate. There is no fixed office, and if anyone other than the owners is involved, it will be on a freelance basis. Many SMEs stay at that point. However, if they do grow further, they will become a Sapling. At the Sapling stage the business has a surplus large enough to fund a fixed office and a small staff role, such as a book-keeper. It is likely now to employ direct staff. If the Sapling continues to grow, then eventually it will become a Tree. Trees are those SMEs that are generating enough of a surplus to allow the owners and initial funders to realise their returns.

We have used this model within our scenarios. In the utopian scenario, the SME concerned had been a successful Sapling and is just on the verge of becoming a Tree. It is just about to become an employer of significance in the area in which it operates. In the dystopian scenario, the business owner managed to push the SME into becoming a Seedling, but, by taking on excessive fixed costs at an early stage, it never really broke through into becoming a Sapling.

Both of the scenarios examine the issue of proximity. One key uncertainty as we move towards 2030 is exactly how important physical transport links are, and the extent to which they can be replaced by a virtual infrastructure. In our utopian scenario, we have assumed a first rate virtual infrastructure for even the remote areas of rural Suffolk by 2030. In this case, really good physical links are an added bonus, but the majority of business takes place on line.

By way of contrast, in our dystopian scenario, we have assumed that the virtual infrastructure is patchy – it is good in populated areas, but not so good in more remote areas – which stress the importance of physical transport links. On top of this, we have assumed that the chronic public under-investment in roads and rail links in Suffolk continues, and, if anything, actually worsens by lengthening travelling times. To a certain extent, we have taken the present and made it more so in the future.

It is our belief that we can act to avoid the dystopian scenario and build the utopian scenario. Two key policy measures and one minor measure stand out in our thinking. First, it is really important to create a thriving SME community. One of the things that business consistently says would encourage this are physical networking opportunities – meetings that are of a social and business nature. When we look at very successful entrepreneurial communities, there is often a club or a group that provides a core focus for that community. There are already in existence in Suffolk a number of organisations that are providing this facility. That there is not a thriving entrepreneurial community suggests that they could do more.

Second, face-to-face networking opportunities are strengthened further if there is the possibility of on-line collaboration between the meetings. For this to occur there has to be a good quality digital infrastructure that SMEs can access. This would mean the roll out of high speed broadband with a sufficiently large bandwidth. Much of the work of the creative sector is produced in digital format and good connectivity is essential to the sharing of ideas. We have put this at the forefront of our utopian scenario.

Of lesser importance are physical transport links. The world of the successful SME that we envisage in 2030 is less to do with moving stuff and more to do with moving ideas and services. In this respect, the key physical items to be moved from one place to another are the people who are travelling from one face-to-face meeting to another. There is an argument in favour of a policy that improves roads, public transport, and which encourages rail freight to replace road freight, but this is of more of a minor consideration when compared to the benefits of building a robust entrepreneurial community and a good digital infrastructure.

In our scenarios, our utopian scenario assumes that the policy mix has been successfully achieved. Our dystopian scenario paints a picture of 2030 in which the current lack of an adequate policy mix continues to lead to an under-achieving entrepreneurial community in Suffolk. The one scenario aims to inspire a different future to our current present, whilst the other serves as a warning against continued complacency in this area.

Lucky Stars

Thursday, 14 November 2030

I hardly know where to begin. I'm writing this journal entry retrospectively as the last week has been utter chaos.

First of all I'm now a mum! The twins were born a week early on the 7th November 2030, a perfect boy and a girl. They're the most beautiful things I've ever seen, just as I imagined they would be, but then they were conceived in the best fertility clinic in Switzerland so I shouldn't sound so surprised[35]. Cost me enough to get them just right, but since the info-tech start up in Silicon Valley IPO'd last year, I cashed out my stock options, so I can afford it[36].

But God it was awful. I've never been so worried in all my life when on Thursday afternoon I went into labour and was rushed into the local NHS hospital. Luckily Josh was with me otherwise I don't know what I would have done. From the first contractions to birth only took four hours! All my plans for a scheduled caesarean in the private hospital in Cambridge went out of the window[37].

The twins went straight into a ventilator to help them with their breathing and I went into hyper-drive. Never thought I'd panic, anyone would tell you how controlled I am (they used to call me the Ice Maiden at school) but I felt so useless and was sedated. I shouldn't have worried because I had made

---

[35] By 2030, we have taken the view that it will be quite common for parents - who have the financial resources - to be able to order the DNA design of their children. We have assumed that a form of genetic engineering will be available to ensure that parents can access the children of their choice.

[36] A key assumption to this scenario is that the current financial system, particularly as operated in the USA, does not undergo a radical overhaul. We have assumed that we retain a 'winner takes all' financial system.

[37] We have assumed that we continue to have the system where private medical treatment is the service delivery of choice. However, when an emergency occurs the service delivery of choice becomes the National Health Service (NHS).

sure that the twins came from a strong gene pool. They didn't let me down. When I came round there were two warm bundles waiting to be fed and from the moment I first held them in my arms my heart melted. Couldn't stop looking them, in fact it's hard to tear myself away but Marika, their nanny, insisted I go and have a rest so here I am. It's wonderful having someone who's so confident with babies. Marika should be, she's brought up seven of her own, including twins, and it's great that her three youngest children have joined her from Latvia[38]. She was so homesick without them; I know I would be if I were parted from my babies. Think I can see the twins stirring on their monitor so I'd better hurry up or it will be time for their next feed.

Anyway enough of baby talk, where should I begin? Oh yes, Thursday morning, before the twins were born would be a good start.

Well I hadn't managed to get much sleep during Wednesday night as indigestion had kept me awake and no matter what position I put myself in none of them were comfortable. Must admit I felt pretty low and wondered if the whole pregnancy thing was worth it, so went to have a pee in the MediLav to see if it could suggest something to pick me up[39]. Turns out I was low in potassium and iron and suggested a breakfast of porridge and banana with a glass of stout followed by a citrus shower. It did make me feel a bit more human, so I checked my emails.

This could have been the reason I went into early labour. The first thing that flashed up was a message from The China Seas Corporation. It read something along the lines of,

---

[38] We have assumed that the UK continues to remain a member of the EU, and that the flow of people between the EU states does not experience a major modification. In this case, it is possible for families to relocate within the EU for work purposes.

[39] We have assumed a smart toilet that analyses urinary deposits and recommends solutions if the contents are seen to be unbalanced. We are suggesting that these could become commonplace in affluent homes by 2030, and would have a wide range of diagnostic uses.

"It is with pleasure that we would like to report that Pendlebury Associates has been awarded the contract to provide avatar services[40] to the executive board of the corporation etc etc."

Imagine that? Me, Amelia Kim, based in Bury St Edmunds, Suffolk, securing a contract with a global organisation based in Shanghai[41]. The Kim dynasty is now assured and it feels so damn good to have proved my detractors wrong.

When I moved out of London three years ago to start up my own business everyone thought I was mad. But I was already in my mid 30s and tired of the fast pace of city life. It felt as though all the life force was being sucked out of me and I hadn't developed a new project in over a year. What I needed was a clean break and to be around a creative bunch of people who had a commitment to their surroundings[42]. Bingo! my luck was in when I found an enterprise hub ten miles out of Bury St Edmunds set on a beautiful arable farm. This enabled me to immerse myself in country life and surround myself with like-minded people; as a result my business took off. It's so easy when you hook up with a networked community.

Coming to Suffolk certainly turned out to be the best thing I could have done and the quality of my life has improved beyond belief[43]. That's not to

---

[40] By 2030, we are suggesting that two trends may come together. First, large volumes of data about us from social media sites are present on-line – not all of them at all flattering. Second, those young people who are uploading material now onto social media sites will have reached a point in their careers where the unflattering material could be something of an embarrassment. Avatar management services are that which locate such data, scrubs it clean, and sanitises the profile history of client.

[41] There are two key assumptions in this story. First, that a new technology to replace the internet has not been developed and has achieved widespread adoption by 2030. This means that a small company based in rural Suffolk can continue to leverage itself as a global player. Second, the promise of high speed broadband in rural Suffolk has finally been delivered at acceptable speeds and bandwidth.

[42] It is our belief that there is a symbiotic link between the Entrepreneurial Community and the Creative Community, and that the key to future prosperity is to be able to combine the two in an appropriate measure. The Entrepreneurs commercialise and monetise the work of the Creatives, and would be lost without them. The Creatives need the Entrepreneurs to commercially exploit the value of their work.

[43] Evidence suggests that the small business community in Suffolk sees it as a great place to live in terms of quality of life. Many small business owners do not have the intention of

say it has all been plain sailing. There have been a few glitches, like the broadband connection in the country was pretty hit and miss and then the enterprise hub folded when the farm where it was located, went under. Relocation was the answer – to my back bedroom! I missed the daily drive out to the country but with all the contacts I had made from my time in the hub, a good broadband connection, and easy access to London by train (in just over 50 minutes[44]), the move did not affect my business. I have to chuckle though when I think back to the presentation I made to The China Seas Corporation; I doubt they would believe that I work from a bedroom in my house! Must remember to thank Dad for spending hours talking to me in Mandarin after I'd finished my homework, I'm sure the executives thought it was my mother tongue[45].

I shouldn't belittle my achievement though as I've been working on this contract for over a year, building up a network of on-line experts from all over the world and bringing them up to speed on avatar management. You wouldn't believe how many top executives (not to mention politicians) have information on the internet that they would rather not be made public. It's great for business – so roll on you bad boys (and girls)!

Of course the first person I contacted when I got the news was Dad, though tracking him down at the university wasn't easy. It never is when he's working on a new project and his fellow dons at Cambridge tend to monopolise his time. Still when I did finally get hold of him he was delighted with my success, but then he always is. Coming from South Korea success is everything.   Then I phoned Mum. Being English her response was more

---

growing their businesses into large scale operations – they are content with a lifestyle business that allows them to earn a living. The internet allows these business owners the opportunity to scale their operations, but they are likely to continue to be lifestyle businesses.

[44] We have assumed that the rail connections between Suffolk and London have improved by 2030. There is some debate over whether good connections would encourage or impede business in Suffolk. We have assumed that they would improve business, but we also acknowledge the contrary arguments.

[45] Our assumption is that China continues to be a dominant player in the global economy and that the ability to communicate directly, even if it is through a filter of technology, will still command a premium in 2030.

muted, her concern was how I would manage such a large contract when I was scheduled to have a caesarean the following week. But that's mum for you. She's more interested in being a grandmother than having a successful daughter[46].

But of course she was right, how would I manage? And for a moment I did doubt myself until I checked my other emails and came across some more good news. It read something like this:

> *"We are delighted to announce that you have been nominated as Business Woman of the Year due to your commitment to developing services that encourage diversity, creativity and innovation through the use of on-line business networking within a rural framework."*

By this time I was breathless with excitement (actually that was probably caused by carrying the huge weight of the twins!) and felt I needed some fresh air to clear my head. Shopping was the answer and I made straight for a new boutique shop with cute baby clothes (yes even more clothes for the twins!), but it seemed that even outside I couldn't escape my success. Flashing across the illuminated hoarding[47] in Market Square was the news of my nomination for Business Women of the Year together with a photograph of me when I went on a trade mission to Singapore[48]. I hoped no-one would recognise me as at that moment I must have looked awful. Then I saw Josh and my heart started pounding.   Still can't believe someone as handsome as him could fall for someone like me, sometimes I have to pinch myself to believe its true. He could have the pick of any

---

[46] We have taken the view that certain cultural traits are unlikely to have changed by 2030. The impact of new technologies may highlight those cultural traits, but change at the cultural level is a lot slower than many reckon it to be.

[47] We envisage a greater use of screen displays in open public spaces in future years. They can be seen currently at places such as railways stations today, but with the reduction of the costs of installing such screens, the improvement of video technologies, and a greater need for more accessible and timely information, the use of public screens could develop significantly by 2030.

[48] It is our view that, despite the networked, on-line, world of 2030, most business will continue to be person-to-person, and that the premium on personal relationships will continue much as it has in previous years. For a global business, it will continue to be as important in 2030 for the business operators to visit their clients as it is today.

gorgeous looking woman, but he says he wants to be with me, despite being pregnant.

I was surprised at how down Josh looked as normally he's so upbeat (I think that is why I like him so much, he's always so positive). He suggested coffee so we went back to my house so I could put my feet up to relieve my swollen ankles. It turned out that, unbeknown to me, Josh had been having a bad time lately. Not only was his Dad ill, but he had just been turned down for a loan from the bank to buy new premises for his business. The answer was obvious, I'd fund the venture[49]. After all I'd done it at Stanford and that'd turned out OK, why not in Suffolk? Anyway I plan for him to be the father of my children so it's in my interest to have him stick around.

Oh, the monitor is flashing big time now. Looks like the twins are ready for their next feed, there's only so much Marika can do before they go full throttle, I'd best close for now.

NOTE - check star charts for missing lucky stars - I'm sure two must have fallen from the sky last Thursday!

---

[49] It was important for us to have some contact between the Entrepreneurial Community and the Creative Community. In this story, the contact comes through the rural hub in which the businesses are co-located. The storyline highlights one of our beliefs that the entrepreneur (Amelia) needs the creative (Josh), and vice-versa. The use of seed funding from one community to the other is a way in which the two can usefully co-operate.

Life's Not Fare – A Taxi Driver's Tale

My life stopped the day the plane fell out of the sky, or at least it felt like it had. At first everyone thought it was a terrorist attack when the aircraft crashed into Canary Wharf, but it turned out to be navigational failure[50]. The whole country came to a standstill and with it my life finally unravelled. That was two years ago.

"Oscar, Bravo, Charlie. Fare for Ipswich Station. Nat can you pick up?"

"Yeh, yeh, I'm here, what else would I be doing on a cold wet January morning? Where's the pick up?"

"I'll GPS it to you[51]. Fare's pretty het up. Apparently all the trains from Woodbridge have been cancelled and he's got a VERY important meeting in London this morning[52]. No doubt thieves have been helping themselves to the copper wiring again[53]."

---

[50] One of the axioms that we are questioning in this scenario is the ability of the automation of life in the future to operate perfectly. In a system of air travel where much of the process of flying is automated, the consequences of a technology failure becomes even greater. The idea of a sat-nav system flying an aeroplane into a tower block may seem fanciful now. We are suggesting that it could become more commonplace in the future.

[51] We have assumed that transport navigational systems will become ubiquitous by 2030. Their cost will have fallen dramatically, making them readily available to small companies as a means of monitoring staff. As long as the technology is functioning, this will give businesses greater control over their staff.

[52] An important assumption in this scenario is that the transport links between Suffolk and London have deteriorated considerably in the years to 2030. We have taken the view, in this scenario, that this will act as a retarding factor to the economic development of Suffolk. It is possible to argue the case the other way – that it acts as a stimulus to the Suffolk economy – but this point is drawn out in other scenarios. In this scenario, we have accepted the conventional wisdom that, as a means to prosperity, Suffolk needs good links to London.

[53] In this scenario we envisage a period of acute resource scarcity. We would expect the scrap price of metals to be high and remain high, which creates a financial incentive to steal copper wiring from rail signalling systems. We also envisage a period where investment in rail signalling systems, particularly in fibre-optic systems, has not occurred.

"Ah well one man's ill-fortune is another man's gain, so they say."

"You could say that.   Talking of another man's gain fancy taking another whipping at poker next Monday?"

"In your dreams. Over and definitely, out."

Mind you if I'm truly honest I could say that my life had been going downhill long before the plane crash, both personally and business wise. The fling with Lucy, my PA, was sheer stupidity and my drinking was so out of control that Summer had no choice but to walk away from our marriage. Took the girls, Tizzy and April, down to her parents in Kent to start a new life, but boy do I miss all of them. Summer had given me so many chances to mend my ways, but I guess she couldn't take any more.

"Oscar, Bravo, Charlie.   Are you there Nat?   This guy is really throwing his teddy bear around. Can't you get a move on?"

"OK OK. It's alright for you in your cosy control room, out here it's raining cats and dogs[54].   Wait I've just picked something up in my headlights. Yes I can see him."

How can I miss him in his blue and red golfing umbrella? What a plonka!

"Hi mate, taxi to Ipswich Station."

"Yes and step to. You'll have to put your foot down if I'm to make the 7.45 am train to London."

Good morning to you too, with your gabardine raincoat and leather briefcase, don't you know that this is 2030 not 1930?   Actually in a funny kind of way this guy reminds me of when I used to have a proper job. It was

---

That leaves us with a situation where there is ample copper wiring to steal and a financial incentive to do so. The result is that the disruption on the rail system is commonplace.

[54] We have assumed that the weather patterns by 2030 have become more extreme than they are now. The current trend of heavier storms that punctuate long dry spells is assumed to continue and worsen, resulting in deluges when it does actually rain. An interesting spin off of this thinking could be to assess the potential impact of climate change upon commuting. However, we saw that as beyond the scope of this project.

the thrill of the chase and the challenge of winning over a new client that got me going. Wasn't always successful mind, but hey you can't win them all. Plan to get back into it again too once I've paid off all my debts[55].

It was great being a boss with my own office, staff, a PA (whom I'd rather forget about) and best of all, getting out there and finding new business. Accountant soon put a stop to all that, told me I was under-capitalised and needed to build more resilience into the business. His idea of building up a client base was through inter-connectivity and not through face to face meetings[56]. What did he know about running a business? Told him that in my line of business you need to make a statement, get noticed, but no he insisted that the company car should go and I foolishly agreed. I should have known he wouldn't stop there, as the next thing he told me to do was to cut my overheads, so I had to get rid of my staff and office. Now all I'm left with is this old jalopy, still a people carrier makes a good taxi.

"What line of business are you in mate, if you don't mind me asking?"

"Personal media enterprises.[57]"

"Is that so? What a coincidence. I used to have my own media consultancy, you might have heard of it, Lempke Marketing?"

"Can't say I have, but then I'm fairly new to this. Got made redundant from my job in The City a year ago and decided to try a new tack[58]. Worked

[55] We envisage that the UK will continue to be an indebted nation to 2030. Prosperity is a key way to resolve the problem of indebtedness. In this scenario we have assumed that growth and prosperity has eluded the UK, and Suffolk in particular, in the years to 2030. In the Entrepreneurial Community, this means that the commercial opportunities available to small businesses are very limited, leading to almost a subsistence type of existence.

[56] A key assumption in this scenario is that there is a premium placed upon using technology - when it is available - to build a client base virtually. We have assumed that the cost of doing business face to face is prohibitive, except where the client insists upon, and is willing to pay for, a more personal service. A structure of low overheads would make for a more resilient business, one that could more readily adapt to changing circumstances.

[57] Personal media enterprises are a service that revolves around the issue of celebrity. We have assumed that everyone – to a greater or lesser extent – has something unique about them. Personal media enterprises is about commercialising this uniqueness and allowing people to gain fully from what makes them special. We see this type of service in demand from corporate executives, politicians, and those in the media.

in finance all my life but after the plane crash in Canary Wharf I re-evaluated my situation and decided to cash in my chips. When the next round of redundancies came along I put my name forward now I work from home, except for today when the damn trains aren't running."

Blasted accountants, can't get away from them, bet he got a nice payoff too. No lucky breaks for me, in fact it's been an uphill struggle from the word go. All started when I was at university and needed money, the Student Union needed some promotional work and I put in a bid for it. The excitement I felt when they chose me was second to none. Natural I was. Still am, if only I didn't have such bad luck.

"Can't we get a move on? My train leaves in 30 minutes."

"Sorry mate the cars are all backed up[59]. I'll cut through at Bell Lane, don't worry I know all the shortcuts."

You'd think with petrol at £15.00 a litre[60] more people would use public transport, but the trouble is the buses are so unreliable and it doesn't help that the High Schools start at 7.30 am. At least it's easier in the afternoon now that schools finish at lunch time.

"Oy, watch where you're going! Did you see that? She could have got herself killed running out in front of me."

---

[58] We have assumed the continued link between Suffolk (a great place to live) and the City of London (a place to earn a salary). It is common for those coming out of the City to establish small businesses in Suffolk. We envisage that this trend will continue as part of the natural demographic churn within the UK. Major incidents tend to accelerate the flow of people from London into Suffolk. This is likely to intensify in the years to 2030.

[59] We have assumed that investment in the local transport infrastructure into Ipswich has been inadequate in the years to 2030. At this point, long delays for short journeys are not uncommon. We have also assumed that investment in alternative public transport options, such as buses, has been limited and ineffective, the result of which has been to exacerbate the dependence upon the car as a means of transport.

[60] In this scenario we have assumed that Peak Oil is real and that it is having a direct impact upon petrol prices. Petrol currently stands at about £1.30 per litre. If inflation ran at 2% per annum (the Bank of England target inflation rate) to 2030, then petrol would be in the region of £1.80 to £2.00 per litre. The gap between this and £15.00 per litre is a statement of how wide the scarcity factor has impacted car travel in this scenario.

Not that the guy in the back would notice with his face stuck in his Sphere. Might have known he would have the latest gadget, those things are amazing, fold down small enough to fit into a shirt pocket yet flexible enough to enlarge to any shape you like[61].

"For God's sake, its 7.30 am, we're never going to make it. Can't you put your foot down?"

"You just sit tight, once we get past this junction, it'll be plain sailing."

Thank goodness Tizzy and April don't have to get up early and go to school, especially on mornings like this. The Local Authority where they live decided to get rid of most of their school buildings and invest in an electronic infrastructure. Beats having to cope with the crowded classrooms they have here[62]. Don't quite understand how it works, but the girls are thriving on it, especially Tizzy who was bullied mercilessly when she was at school here and April is a genius with technology. Mind you I do miss them; the most I can manage is to snatch a couple of hours here and there which isn't the same as seeing them every day. Working weekends and nights is the only way you can make a living in this line of work, still I usually pop down and see them for an hour or two after taking a fare to Heathrow or Gatwick.

Funny, looking at him in the back of my cab takes me back a few years. I'd forgotten about how stressful it is rushing to a meeting.

"It must be difficult working on your own without the infrastructure of an office?"

---

[61] We have assumed a technology that is flexible and portable, that is interconnected and has much larger data capacities than we currently enjoy. We see this technology as relatively ubiquitous in the small business sector by 2030.

[62] We have drawn a distinction between Suffolk and Kent in terms of education. In Suffolk, we have assumed an educational framework that is traditional in its approach. There are classrooms, teachers, and a relatively low tech environment. The consequence of this is that classrooms are crowded and there are problems in transporting children between home and school. Kent, by way of contrast, has opted for an electronic infrastructure, where lessons are delivered on-line. This captures a current debate in the world of futurists: to what extent will future education be on-line?

"Not at all, in fact it's been very liberating. Who needs to travel to an office when you can build networks across the world from the comfort of your favourite armchair? I'm only going to all this effort today as the client insisted on meeting at his club in Soho. We could have done everything on Skype[63]. Only yesterday I signed up an NGO in Africa[64], the fact that it was a Sunday makes no difference to me."

"But surely you'd prefer to see the person you are working for, get a feel for what they want?"

"Not really. I can do all my research via my laptop and speak to them via Skype conference."

"Just be careful that you're not undercut from Asia like I was. How could I compete with kids with no overheads other than a connection to the web?[65]"

"You're right, it's a challenge but I decided not to deal in the mass market, instead I work in a niche economy providing a tailor made service to high earners. I've made plenty of contacts over the years now I'm capitalising on them.[66]"

---

[63] Our point here is that, by 2030, we have assumed that a face to face meeting will have become something of an expensive luxury, and that it is far more common to be building business relationships on-line.

[64] This reflects our view that, in order to be successful in 2030, a small business would have to be naturally global in its vision. Africa is currently an area with enormous potential, and we have assumed that, by 2030, some of that potential will be realised.

[65] This point highlights the extent to which we see the business world becoming more global in its orientation by 2030, and the inroads that low cost economies, such as those in Asia, could make into the service sector by that time. If the business world does go on-line, it creates threats as well as opportunities. In this case, the threat from low cost competitors has forced Lempke Marketing out of business.

[66] We have assumed that the key to future success for small business lies in the ability to move up the value chain in the services they provide by finding a high value niche, and to be able to leverage a network of contacts in doing so. By 2030, we have assumed that this ability will be critical at both an individual and community level.

Never get me hiding behind some networked technology like this loner, no I'd much rather be out there meeting people. Thank goodness I'll soon be rid of him he's beginning to get on my nerves.

"Here we are mate, Ipswich Station, and with five minutes to go before your train. Not bad, eh? That'll be £49.50 please.[67]"

"I've only got a £50.00 note, so you might as well keep the change."

Smug geezer, might have guessed he wouldn't be a big tipper.

"Oscar, Bravo, Charlie, where are you Nat?"

"Just dropped my fare at Ipswich Station."

"Lady wants a ride to London. Apparently there's a signal failure at Manningtree and all trains to London have been cancelled."

---

[67] It is almost axiomatic that higher base resource prices will feed into higher prices for the services provided using those resources. There is a subtle point at work here. Currently, taxi fares are about four times the cost of the base resource input. In this scenario, taxi prices have fallen to about three times the base resource input. This suggests a reduction in the real incomes of service providers in the years to 2030, and suggests that Suffolk is likely to become even more impoverished than it is now.

CHAPTER 4

THE CARING COMMUNITY

As we move towards 2030, two features of the journey are likely to be continued austerity in the public sector and the ageing of the population in Suffolk. The Caring Community occupies the intersection between those two trends, which is why we found it to be so interesting. Traditionally, the care focus has been upon the education of the young, the social care of the old, and the healthcare of society as a whole. We are living at a time when these definitions are blurring and the traditional compartments for social care no longer work as well.

The boundaries of public and private provision are currently changing. The private sector has a greater role to play in activities formerly undertaken by the public sector. Normally, the key driver of this change is the need to provide more services at a lower cost. We are moving into a model of provision where the public sector commissions - and pays for - the social care, which is then delivered – by contract – through a private sector provider. Continued restrictions on public spending are likely to see this trend continue for many years to come.

This trend, however, is not without risk. There are two key uncertainties to the policy – uncertainty over the quality of service and uncertainty over delivery. There are many who suspect that the cost of provision of public services is reduced by sacrificing their quality. Indeed, those who advocate this view can point to recent scandals in privately run care homes, where the policy of providing care at the lowest cost is alleged to not have been of an acceptable standard. As the numbers of the dependent elderly increase to 2030, it is not hard to foresee a number of political scandals around the issue of social care for the elderly.

The uncertainty over delivery hinges around market failure. Those who hold this view would remind us all that companies can become insolvent, either through bad luck, pure mismanagement, poor financing or whatever source. If a private care provider ceases to operate, their beneficiaries will still need provision, and it will be the public sector which has to intervene to bail out the private sector failure. In its present format, the partnership between public commissioners and private providers places all of the contractual risk upon the public sector. It is not beyond the realm of possibility to foresee this situation changing, possibly through the use of financial instruments such as performance bonds or failure insurance.

There is an overlay of technology that we can add to complicate the picture. The direction of technology is to allow our personal devices to become smaller, faster, more connected, and cheaper to run. This has the potential to revolutionise the way in which care is delivered in a very short timeframe. So far, it has given rise to more distributed forms of care delivery as patients take responsibility for financing their diagnostic equipment (the smart phone) and moving the point of delivery of care away from a centralised unit and further into the home, a trend that has a great deal of momentum as we move out to 2030. By this time, it is entirely possible that a good part of education, eldercare, and healthcare are delivered in the home. If this happens, then it raises questions about our current investments of equipment and buildings in centralised delivery services. The process of disintermediation has the potential to significantly alter the way in which care is delivered.

We wanted our scenarios of the possible future to capture these three themes (a) the intersection of the two major trends - the ageing society and further fiscal retrenchment, (b) the idea of the abandonment of quality in care provision – either through design or market failure, and (c) an overlay of technology that allows for more distributed care provision.

Our utopian scenario is based around an episode of child care. In it, two sisters and their mother face an enormous number of difficulties within the home, at school, and at work. We have tried to get away from the stigma of the undeserving poor by posing them as the innocent victims of a set of tragic circumstances. The care response is co-ordinated and interlocking. We have imagined agencies working with each other rather than against each other, trying to get the best result for the family rather than protecting budgets. We have imagined one further point, which is that a rudimentary form of social investment appraisal informs policy actions, the focus of which is to help the family, and the individuals within it, to become fully contributing members of society. Without trying to reduce the issue to a monetary calculus, it is based on the belief that if you help people to better themselves, then that is exactly what they will do.

The dystopian scenario is a future to be avoided. This is an exaggeration of how we see current trends moving over the next couple of decades. The story line is around an episode of end-of-life care. As society ages, this issue is likely to become ever more pressing. We have imagined a world in which the nursing staff are too burdened with too much work to care for their patients, with the resulting consequences of confusion, dehydration, and starvation within hospitals. We have taken the current episodic occurrences of this, and made it widespread in 2030. In this world, the hospital is a place to be feared. It is the place where most people die, unloved and not cared for, in tragic and horrible circumstances. We have also underlined the point that, whilst this is the experience of end-of-life care for most people, those with adequate financial resources can buy a better level of care. We feel that this two-tier system is likely to suffer greater inspection as we move out to 2030.

It is said that a key measure of equity in society is how its vulnerable members are treated. We wanted our scenarios to act as a catalyst in a debate about future care platforms. In particular, we see two important issues for the future. First, to what degree will we see organisational change that puts the beneficiary of care at the centre of the care process? Our utopian scenario shows what could be possible in this area, whilst the dystopian scenario gives a view of how things can be if we continue on our current path.

The second issue concerns whether are we willing to see even greater divergence in the experience of care, based upon the ability to pay? Our dystopian scenario gives a vision of a world in which there is less equality than there is today. It is not a better world. Our utopian scenario, on the other hand, takes its inspiration from the beginning of the welfare state in the UK. There is something inspiring from this part of our history. It is seen as a time when the whole nation was really in it together. When there was a great deal of social cohesion and social justice.

One aspect of sustainability that is often overlooked is the need to operate a fair and just society. The definition of what is fair varies between communities and changes over time. However, it is usually the case that an equitable solution should be reached as a pre-requisite for a well-balanced society. Many argue that we are a long way from that point currently. However, that doesn't mean we couldn't be there in 2030. To this extent, we are optimistic about the future

CONFIDENTIAL PSYCHOLOGICAL REPORT

Review Meeting to assess the progress of twin sisters

Pavla & Raina Hinova

Surname of Children: Hinova   **Other Names: Pavla & Raina**

Date of Birth: 9 June 2022   Sex: Female

Chronological Age: 8 years 4 months

Present School: St Giles Primary School

Date of Visit: 10 October 2030

Name and address of person with parental responsibility:

Mrs Galina Hinova, 32 Shirley Road, Ipswich, Suffolk, IP3 9DJ

Attending

Mrs Galina Hinova	Parent
Mrs Herbert	Class Teacher
Bronwyn Jeffreys	Special Educational Needs Coordinator
Robert Miller	Educational Psychologist

Background to referral

Twin sisters, Pavla and Raina, were referred to the Educational Psychology Service in December 2029 following consultation with their teacher, Mrs Herbert, and Special Educational Needs Officer, Bronwyn Jeffreys, at a Planning Meeting held at St Giles Primary School. The meeting highlighted particular concerns in the areas of the girls' behaviour, attention, concentration, speech and social interaction difficulties. It was decided that the girls would be assessed by an educational psychologist. This report is to review the progress made since the last assessment was carried out on 12 December 2029.

The family arrived in Suffolk in 2027 after witnessing the murder of Mr Hinova, the girls' father, in a suspected gangland killing[68]. It is alleged that Mr Hinova's death was one in a number of revenge killings by a criminal gang seeking to maintain their presence in that area. Mr Hinova had the misfortune of being associated with a rival gang through his involvement as a taxi driver to the wife of a leading member of a rival gang. He was killed as a consequence of this association.

Fearful that the killers might widen their net and return to seek out Mrs Hinova and the girls; they fled the family home in Bulgaria to seek refuge with her brother, the girls' uncle, in Ipswich. All members of the family were in a state of extreme trauma and it was agreed that help be offered to them.

Conclusions of Psychological Report dated 12 December 2029

The report outlined that the family were in need of help both of a physical and mental capacity and the following services were recommended[69]:

- Individual and group counselling sessions with Children's Mental Health Services.
- Referral to Adult Mental Health Services for Mrs Hinova.
- An individual Education Plan drawn up for Pavla and Raina to assess their educational needs.

---

[68] Our assumption is, by 2030, that the United Kingdom will remain in the European Union, that Bulgarian citizens will be able to move freely within the EU, and that Bulgaria will continue to have issues with organised criminal gangs. Each of these three assumptions could be called into question.

[69] We have assumed that the local care services are able to operate an integrated approach to the care package offered the family, and that the agencies involved operate in a co-ordinated fashion to pool resources for each case. Care is currently delivered by an array of providers and agencies, who may or may not operate in a co-ordinated way. It is our assumption that, by 2030 there will be a greater degree of co-operation than at present and that the focus of care will be upon those receiving it.

- Anger management therapy sessions are made available to help Pavla deal with her anger issues.
- Allocation of a Family Support Worker to help the family with adapting to life in a strange country.
- Referral to Housing as the family is currently living in one room in the uncle's house.
- Access to English language classes for Mrs Hinova.

Current Situation as at 10 October 2030

Pavla and Raina are now highly supported in school. With the services of an interpreter, the school have managed to engage the support of Mrs Hinova who was, at first, withdrawn and suspicious of any attempts to offer help to the family. All members of the family have stated that they miss their family and friends in Bulgaria.

Raina Hinova

Of the two girls the biggest improvement has been seen in Raina who has responded well to intensive counselling and play sessions. At first Raina was withdrawn and would curl into a ball at the back of the class to avoid all contact with either school staff or other children in her class. She exhibited profound psychological trauma by constant scratching resulting in deep gashes on her arms and legs. At home Raina would wet the bed and suffered nightmares, screaming when her mother left the room. It is believed that Raina was sitting on her father's lap watching television when he was shot twice in the chest and once in the head. She was found covered in blood hiding under a coffee table by her mother and did not speak for a year after the event.

Raina has now regained her speech and taken to learning English well. She is confident enough to part with her mother before joining the class line up at the start of school and walk quietly into class. The scratching has stopped and she interacts well with her class and has a small friendship group.

Raina has been placed within a class of supportive peers and has the support of a Linguist Assistant who speaks several languages, including Bulgarian[70]. As a result Raina has developed a good command of the English language and is able to communicate her thoughts and feelings in a controlled manner. She still needs one to one support to help to remain on-task as Raina can easily become withdrawn and lose concentration, but is happy to work in small groups.

Pavla Hinova

Pavla is the more dominant of the two girls and can, at times, be over protective of her sister. This can cause conflict between the two girls when Raina does not want such attention. It is believed that Pavla was playing in her bedroom at the time of her father's murder and has stated that she feels angry that she let her family down by not being there to help protect her father.

Pavla has a limited understanding of English which leads to frustration causing her to lose her temper and shout in her native language, often frightening the other members of her class, who needed a counselling intervention. At first it was left to Raina to calm her sister down until a 'Time Out' strategy was implemented. This means when Pavla feels she is losing her temper she will take a green card to the class teacher and be escorted to The Curve where a dedicated team of multi lingual support teachers manage children from a number of ethnic backgrounds with their challenging behaviours[71]. Originally this was happening several times a day, but this has now fallen back to once or twice a week. Pavla also

---

[70] We have assumed that a greater set of language skills has become available to the care sector by 2030. As the population of Europe moves from one area to another, the issue of language skills becomes more pressing. As a result, we have assumed that more resources are put into language training in the years to 2030, particularly in classroom settings, with effect of ensuring that language is no longer a barrier to learning.

[71] We have assumed that, by 2030, it is accepted that there are greater benefits to society if anti-social behaviour is remediated at an early stage in a child's development rather than allowing it to take root in a child's behaviour. As a consequence, resources are put into schools to allow the child to develop without this anti-social behaviour.

attends an anger management sessions run by the school nursing team at Totten Clinic and this has given her coping strategies for when she is out of school and this has improved home life[72].

Galina Hinova - Mother

After overcoming the language barrier and her distrust of authority, Mrs Hinova has responded well to counselling sessions with the Adult Mental Health Services.

A Family Support Worker has been allocated to the family enabling Mrs Hinova to access English language classes, register with a GP, complete the necessary paperwork to obtain a National Insurance Number, and to apply for those benefits to which she is eligible, including liaising with the local borough council to obtain a council house[73]. The family are now living in a two-bedroom house and Mrs Hinova has a part time job working in the kitchens of St Peter's High School utilising her skills as a chef[74].

Furthermore, it was discovered by the Family Support Worker that as a result of Mrs Hinova being knocked unconscious at the time of her husband's murder, she sustained a broken arm. This was not treated in Bulgaria because Mrs Hinova was desperate to get away from the family home. She did not say anything when she first arrived in England because she was afraid that the children would be taken away from her if anyone

---

[72] We have assumed a far greater deal of co-operation between the Education Services, the Social Services, and the National Health Service than presently operates. His goes beyond the co-operation of staff, and includes the integration of care systems, the development of integrated records, and the inter-changeability of staff from one care setting to another.

[73] We have assumed that a programme of building publicly funded social housing is undertaken by 2030, resulting in accommodation at fair rents that is readily available to priority cases. In many cases, the key to effective intervention in social care is adequate and affordable housing. This currently falls under a number of jurisdictions and a major improvement in the delivery of social care would be to integrate the inputs of each agency involved in any one case.

[74] We have assumed that the purpose of social care is to facilitate the individual and family becoming a fully functioning member of society. We used the working assumption that most recipients do not want to be reliant upon state aid and that the poverty trap – where people are worse off when moving from benefits to work – has been resolved effectively by 2030.

found out what had happened. The result was that Mrs Hinova was in constant pain causing her to have a low temper threshold. Corrective surgery was carried out at the beginning of the summer holidays followed by a two-week stay at Heathlands, a residential respite centre for patients with dependent children[75]. The girls attended the play sessions attached to the centre allowing the family to spend time together and have a holiday, whilst giving Mrs Hinova the chance to recuperate from her operation. In addition the family attended group therapy sessions which allowed the family time to grieve and come to terms with the death of Mr Hinova, something they had not had the opportunity to do before.

Discussion with School

Mrs Herbert, class teacher, spoke very positively about Raina and Pavla, stating that their behaviour has improved significantly since the girls started at the school a year and a half ago. Raina is one of the quieter members of the class but contributes well when working in small groups. Pavla, on the other hand, is more vocal but does not always make herself understood resulting in aggressive and loud behaviour. Since the introduction of the 'Time Out' card, Pavla has been more in control of her emotions and, once she has calmed down, has proved to be an eager and attentive learner. Both girls are currently working at below average ability but this is to be expected considering the fact that they missed nearly a year at school.

Summary

Over the last ten months the girls have made pleasing progress and are responding well to the measures put in place to support them. Raina, although still quiet, has become more confident and no longer displays her disturbing scratching behaviour. While Pavla, by learning to manage her

---

[75] We have assumed a system of patient centred social care that integrates education, social services, and the National Health Service. Critical to this is the timing of the delivery of healthcare at a point suitable for the patient, and, as the opportunity is available, the delivery of a number of complementary services at the same time.

temper, is displaying signs that she is very bright and eager to learn[76]. It is important, however, to continue to monitor the girls' behaviour and would suggest that a further development check of Raina and Pavla's needs be carried out in six months time.

Recommendations

- Staff to continue to support Raina and Pavla with developing appropriate behaviours within the classroom. This will include prompting Pavla to sit on the carpet during group discussion and the use of a visual timetable for both Pavla and Raina to ensure they understand what is happening in class.

- The use of the sensory room to enable Raina and Pavla to connect with their life in Bulgaria, incorporating 3-D sights and sounds of their home town in Bulgaria[77].

- Access to social skills groups such as Time to Talk and continue with the work of developing an understanding of feelings using a 'Box of Feelings' as well as the use of hand puppets.

- Family Support Worker to encourage Mrs Hinova to integrate into local life and develop her own support network.

- Counselling sessions with Child Mental Health Services to be reviewed with a view to reducing the sessions to once every two weeks.

- Mineral supplements are given to the girls to help boost their concentration[78].

---

[76] Central to this scenario is the belief that the purpose of social care is to bring out the best of everyone in society and to give them ample opportunity to use fully all of their gifts. It is our belief that children represent an investment in our collective futures, and that it makes good sense for us all to encourage the best in all children.

[77] We have assumed a greater use of more developed Information Technology within the school in the years to 2030. This implies that the necessary infrastructure investments in the years leading to 2030 have been undertaken and are well bedded in.

[78] This touches upon the thorny issue of performance enhancing medication within the school system. We have assumed that our current fears about this medication have proved to be unfounded by 2030, that the use of the prescribed medications is not uncommon, and that the benefits of such a programme are widely open to all.

- Tab computers to be allocated to Raina and Pavla to enable them to access the school's on-line learning programme. This will enable the girls to improve their educational attainment which is currently below their ability. Their progress will be monitored by The Learning Development Team at the school[79].
- Local authority to fund broadband connectivity at home to facilitate access to on-line learning modules.

Date of Next Review Meeting

To be held at St Giles School in three months time on 10 January 2031.

---

[79] We have assumed that, by 2030, text books will have largely disappeared, to be replaced by computing devices that are integrated on-line. In some circumstances, low achieving pupils can be put upon a catch up programme, delivered from home, using devices given to them by the school.

Lost In Time

I don't remember what was said in the confusion of that meeting with the doctor, all I can recall is Josh losing his temper and storming out of the room. He came back a few minutes later, mind, and I could tell he had been crying from his bloodshot eyes, but after that it was all a blur. The next thing I knew I was waking up in a room full of strangers, took me ages to work out where I was, it did. It was probably the smell that gave it away and made me realise I was no longer at home, but funnily enough the pungent smell of body fluids mixed with antiseptic took me back to when I was a young boy[80].

"Can't help herself, poor deary," I recall my mother saying. "When you get old you lose control over your body, need someone to look after you, you do, and we're here to look after Granny aren't we, Phillip?"

Every morning Mum would clear away the soiled sheets so that by the time I took Granny in her breakfast, the room had transformed into a haven of violets and lavender. How Mum coped I've no idea - especially after Dad was killed while bailing hay – it can't have been easy bringing up four children, running a farm and looking after a bed bound Granny. Give anything to hear Mum's voice again, I would, but doubt I'll get to see her now she's is living in a care home in Felixstowe near my sister. It was always a family joke that Mum would outlive us all, looks like we were right, at 105 she still has all her faculties and enjoys outings to the Spa Theatre and walks along the prom. Perhaps I should have given up the farm earlier and gone to live by the sea.

---

[80] We have assumed that one of the constants between the past, present, and future is the smell of a hospital. When thinking of the future, one can readily focus upon what changes there will be. However, we also need to think about those things that will not change.

Mum was right though, when you get old you do lose control of your body, well at least the unlucky ones like me do[81].   If I hadn't developed lung cancer I'd still be out there working the land, but this hacking cough stops me from doing anything and as soon as I move the pain spreads down the back into my legs.   Mind you even with all this pain I could murder for a cigarette, since I've been confined to bed I've not been able to have one. Sometimes I can't work out which is worse, the craving for a cigarette or the pain.   Josh, bless him, used to quietly wheel me off the hospital grounds[82], but I can't even manage that now as sitting in one position has become too painful, all I can do is lie on my back.

It's the losing control that I hate the most, not just control over my body but control over my life.   At least Granny managed a glass of her favourite tipple on the day she died.   Mum told me it would have been her wedding anniversary if Grandpa had been there; she said they had always celebrated it with champagne.   Stayed with me all my life it has, Granny passing away peacefully in her own bed, hoped I would go like that but that's not likely to happen now[83].

I don't blame Josh.   He wasn't given any support from the medicals and did his best to nurse me through my chemotherapy, what with its side-effects and all, but it got to the point where he just couldn't cope. Or maybe it was that I couldn't bear having Josh clear up after me.   I've always been so

---

[81] The question of the dependent elderly is likely to become more pressing as we move to the year 2030. In this scenario, we have assumed that not a great deal has changed in models of care, except for the levels of funding, which have progressively reduced over the intervening periods. The scene is set where there are larger numbers of the dependent elderly at a time when the resources per patient are at historical lows.

[82] We have assumed that the National Health Service will take responsibility for end of life care by 2030. There is an argument that Social Services ought to have an input, but this scenario assumes that Social Services will divest itself of all budgetary responsibility for each case at the earliest opportunity.

[83] We have tried to capture the mechanisation of the end of life process by 2030, where the interests of the patient are subservient to the interests of the care provider. It is a de-humanised system, where the process has a feel of a conveyor belt, to maximise throughput and to minimise cost per intervention. We see the language of care becoming the language of the accountant.

strong, see, had to be when my wife, Margaret, passed away following complications after Peter was born. Bitter sweet time that was, the birth of another son and the loss of my beloved wife, don't think I'll ever get over it. Still I'm so proud of my sons, the first children in our family to go to university, even though the cost of it almost ruined us[84]. Just hope I live long enough to see Peter graduate next year. The boys have done me and Margaret proud and at least I have my memories to fall back on, something I do a lot of these days.

"Good Morning, Mr Godbold, time for breakfast. I'll just leave it here on the table for you."

I wait for the clatter to subside before opening my eyes. The ward hands don't hang around for long, they've too much to do, so they keep saying. Josh gets mad at them when he comes to visit and finds my bed all crumpled with me sitting in my own mess[85]. At least with my eyes closed I can forget I'm in hospital and block out the sight of the other inmates. 'God's waiting room' I've heard the nurses say, sometimes I wish my waiting was over, not much point in hanging around if I can't do anything.

When I finally open my eyes I try to focus but can only make out a blur in front of me. Looks like toast and tea again for breakfast, what I could do with a steaming bowl of porridge or a plate of bacon and eggs. Not that I have the stomach for that now, but I used to enjoy a hearty breakfast after putting in a couple of hours work. Yes it's definitely toast, I can smell it. Find it hard to see anything since my glasses disappeared and it doesn't

---

[84] In this scenario, we have assumed that the marketisation of education continues to 2030. We have assumed that the cost of a tertiary education becomes even more prohibitive than it is now. This implies that the spiralling cost of education continues to rise, and that the bubble in the cost of education does not burst.

[85] Despite the political rhetoric to the contrary, we have assumed that there is no real political will to resolve the lack of basic care in the NHS in the years to 2030. Whilst governments continue to be embarrassed by patients dying from thirst and hunger whilst in hospital, it remains the case that there is not the political will to fund adequate levels of staffing to remedy this situation.

help that my vision is often blurred[86]. Suppose it's my fault as I've not told anyone that I've lost my specs and can't see, but I don't want to trouble Josh as he has just started up a new business in the village and has trouble enough of his own. I try to eat the soggy white toast but my appetite eludes me, more than anything I'd love a drink of tea, but don't trust myself not to spill it. Looking at the other shapes in the beds, I'd say it's the same for all the men on the ward, if only there was someone to offer a bit of help I'm sure more food would be eaten. Take old George opposite me, he was 102 yesterday but there was no celebration and I've never seen him eat anything. His wife passed away last week and goodness knows where his family is, they certainly don't come to visit. Doubt he'll last the day but then that is probably a blessing as I reckon he must have bed sores from lying in one position so long. I should know, I've got one on my left buttock. The nurses rarely change his sheets or give him a bed bath[87]. Too busy I suppose.

"Not hungry this morning, Mr Godbold? Let me take your plate for you. The doctor will be round later to see you."

I try to ask for some water but my mouth is so dry that nothing comes out and the orderly is gone before I have the chance to make myself heard. I envy him the ability to move so quickly and wish I still had the vitality of the young, it's as though all the energy has been sapped out of me, like a leaf shrivelling up in the autumn. It's especially hard as, before the cancer hit me, I'd hardly had a day off through ill health in my life. Working the land means you always have fresh air, could never understand how anyone would want to work in an office breathing in everyone else's germs.

---

[86] We have assumed that basic levels of care are not being delivered in hospitals. In this scenario, the patient does not have his spectacles – so he has problems seeing what is given him – and that his dentures have been lost when moving him between wards – inhibiting his ability to eat. None of the care staff have the time to look for them.

[87] In writing this scenario, we have taken current examples of lack of care in the NHS, and we have exaggerated them in the years to 2030. It is our view that the current health system is overly process focussed and insufficiently patient focussed. A key assumption of this scenario is that this situation worsens in the years to 2030.

"Dad, visiting time is about to come to an end and I'm going to have to go. I don't want to get into an argument again with the nurses, you know how shirty they get if the visitors stay later than the allotted time.[88]"

Is it visiting time again? Time has no meaning for me as I drift in an out of consciousness and voices filter through my head as I recall events that happened in the past. Dad shouting from the sideline when I scored my first goal in the under 11s football team, Margaret's sweet voice when she said she would marry me, Josh's cry as I held him for the first time. The voices carry on into a lifetime of memories.

"Dad, can you hear me? I've got to go."

Summoning up all my energy I open my eyes to see Josh looking down at me. I offer a smile, though I get the feeling that it looks more like a grimace as my dry lips try to part over empty gums. Goodness knows what happened to my dentures. Josh bends over me and his concerned look worries me. I try to voice my fears about the future and how he will manage and how he must look after his brother when I'm gone.

"Calm down Dad, there's no need to get agitated, Milly's here with me," I hear Josh say. "We've managed to track the consultant down this afternoon and told her that we're taking you home tomorrow. She wasn't happy, but it's all been arranged. You'll have a team of dedicated nurses and a room overlooking Ten Acre Field. You'll be home in time to celebrate Christmas.[89]"

---

[88] We have assumed that, in this healthcare system, relatives of the patients are seen as disturbances to be endured by the system. We wanted to highlight how every element within the healthcare system is directed towards serving it, and disturbances to the system are tolerated, but not embraced. The interest of a family in the progress of a patient is seen as unwelcome and unnecessary.

[89] It is central to this scenario that we highlight the common experience of end of life care. We also wanted to make the point that those who can afford a better solution will be able to buy just that. A key assumption here is that we, as a society, continue to tolerate a two tier health system to 2030 and that the key determinant between the two is the ability to pay for a better one.

Is it Christmas already? I thought it was still the summer.

"The doctor didn't want to sign you off, but Milly laid into them after she got hold of your notes and realised just how far they had been neglecting you.   Goodness knows when you last had something to eat.[90]"

I think back to the time Josh took me to meet his current lady friend, Amelia, or Milly as he calls her. She'd prepared my favourite meal, rack of lamb followed by sherry trifle. It's a great comfort to know that Josh has found someone he wants to settle down with, I hope Peter will do the same when he finishes university.

"Old Mr Godbold's dreaming again," the nurse laughs as I feel a sharp prick in the top of my arm.

From behind closed eyelids I sense the lights being dimmed as the staff change for the night and calm settles through the ward.   As the pain subsides I feel myself lost in time looking out over Ten Acre Field where the heady scent of ripe corn wafts towards me.

"Won't be long before harvesting," I hear myself say not expecting anyone to hear me until I spot a familiar figure walking through the corn towards the coppice on the far end of the field. "Margaret, wait for me," I cry as I see my beloved wife.

Margaret turns, her warm smile drawing me to her. "It's been too long, I'm home now."

---

[90] One of the things that we excluded from this scenario, but could well have included, was the possibility of a law suit against the healthcare provider for negligence. It would not have added much to the story. However, we do feel that claims for medical negligence are likely to rise substantially in the years to 2030 as healthcare providers are held to account.

CHAPTER 5

THE COASTAL COMMUNITY

At first sight, the Coastal Community might seem to be an odd choice for our attention. The geographical borders of Suffolk are predominantly land based. And yet the coast is important in how Suffolk views itself. There is a history of trade along the rivers and estuaries of Suffolk, with many of the main settlements within the county developing along the water borne trade routes. The impact of rain, wind, and tide is also likely to change in the years to 2030, which could result in a change to the delicate balance of land use that has previously been enjoyed.

It is expected that disruptive climate change could start to become evident within the next twenty years. The disruptions caused by climate change are likely to manifest themselves through changes to the water cycle. Rainfall could become more extreme, whilst long periods where no rain falls also become manifest. For those communities based on the coast this could imply threats from both river flooding and from tidal flooding resulting from stormier weather.

It is unlikely that coastal communities will experience an inundation from the sea due to rising sea levels by 2030. In this time, the level of the sea can be expected to rise by about 6cm on average, which suggests that stories of parts of the coast becoming islands are something of an exaggeration. The root of this exaggeration lies in our inability to think in climactic timescales. A far more likely case is that the processes of sea erosion and deposition may act to reposition the coastline over this period.

The Suffolk coast ought not to be seen as a homogenous entity. Parts of the coast have a high industrial value, whilst others have a high residential value. And yet again, parts of the coast have been scheduled to be abandoned to the sea on the grounds that the cost of sea defence is far higher than the economic value of the land to be protected. Whilst this may be an argument of economic efficiency, it is hardly likely to be seen as a good solution in terms of community equity. It is by no means certain that we have an adequate structure to balance the needs of equity and efficiency at present. This is unlikely to change too much as we go into the future.

It is also the case that, when we view the water cycle throughout Suffolk, a high degree of externality exists within current and future land use patterns. The construction of residential property on river flood plains has led to a much faster throughput of high rainfall onto coastal communities. The investment to protect the downstream communities from high peaks of river flow hasn't been adequate for the job required, leaving the coastal communities to pay the cost of upstream residential development. There is a case for a greater sensitivity to downstream impacts when planning applications are considered by the planning authorities.

The issue of the water cycle and the Suffolk coastal communities is one that is dominated by externalities. It calls into question what economic efficiency means and leads us to ask where equity fits into that calculation. As we move into the future, we can expect key parts of the infrastructure, which reflect a different weather cycle, to be placed under severe strain. It is by no means evident that sufficient funds will be made available to fill those gaps in infrastructure, which suggests that we can expect the number of disruptive events to occur more regularly as time goes by.

We wanted our scenarios about the coastal community to catch the flavour of this dilemma. If the balance of land use changes, it will be to the benefit of some and to the detriment of others. In this, we wanted to capture our belief that the future is generally neutral. When change happens, some find nothing but opportunity within it, whilst others find nothing but challenges.

Central to both scenarios is disruptive climate change. To a certain extent, we could see this disruption as a process whereby we move from one established weather pattern to another. What is important here is the speed at which this change might happen and what actions we can take now to prepare for it. As there will clearly be those who benefit from change and those who lose from it, there is an argument in terms of fairness for some redistributive mechanism to temper the gains and to mitigate some of the losses.

The utopian scenario – Bountiful Blowers - is based around the experience of someone who can adjust to a world changing around him. Within the changes that he experiences, he sees a number of opportunities and is able to capitalise upon them. This is very important for coastal communities such as Lowestoft, which currently experiences higher than average unemployment, poverty, and deprivation. For the community to renew itself, then members of that community will have to provide leadership for renewal. It is unlikely to come from external sources. We have written into the story a character with great vision and optimism for the future, someone who is prepared to inspire the community into renewal.

Our dystopian scenario – Walking Round In Circles – looks at some of the costs to the community caused by change. Most of these costs come in the form of negative externalities – people who suffer loss from the process of change. There is an argument that those who enjoy the positive externalities of change should compensate those losing from it for their loss. That mechanism is absent at present, and we have assumed that it continues to be absent. Based in Orford, a little further south along the coast to Lowestoft, it tells the story of someone whose life changes for the worse. There is little in the way of off-setting the negative externality that she receives from change, which triggers something of a downward spiral for her. In many respects, this is a future that we ought to be working upon to avoid.

The scenarios are based upon a macro-future, one which we can do little to influence directly, and which we can only prepare for. Central to the subject of macro-futures is the issue of externalities and how the benefits can be shared more evenly, with the disbenefits being borne more fairly. We currently do not have the right balance here. Our challenge is to find a better structure as we move into the future.

Obituary for Thomas Blowers

Master Seaman, Father and Visionary

January 18 1942 – October 31 2030

Thomas Blowers, known locally as Bountiful Blowers, died peacefully, aged 88, at home surrounded by his family. An experienced seaman whose life was dominated by the sea, he will be sorely missed by everyone who knew him[91].

Thomas was born in Lowestoft, the son of a fisherman, where from an early age he developed his love of the sea. The youngest of five brothers, he left school at 15 to join the merchant navy as a cadet and worked his way up through the ranks to become a master mariner. Although he travelled extensively for much of his life Thomas always thought of Lowestoft as his home, returning every year to see his family. In 1968 he married Poppy Hills, his childhood sweetheart, and set up home in Kessingland. The couple went on to have three children.

Drama was never far away from Thomas's life. In the late 1980's his career in the merchant navy came to an abrupt end when, whilst captaining a cruise ship in the Indian Ocean, terrorists overran his ship killing two passengers in the process. In an act of bravery which earned him The George Cross, the highest award of gallantry for a civilian, Thomas offered himself as hostage in an effort to avoid any further bloodshed. After several days of tense negotiation, the incident was resolved without any further loss of life. This brush with death caused Thomas to take stock of his life and in 1989 his seafaring life came to an end when he took up a position as a pilot

---

[91] Our thanks go to John West, who gave us invaluable assistance over the nautical details of this scenario. We have tried to make these as accurate as possible. Any shortfall in this regard is entirely due to our misunderstanding of the facts.

for the Port of Lowestoft and volunteered for the RNLI as coxswain of the Kessingland lifeboat.

Settling into family life did not come easy to Thomas as he was used to vast oceans and periods of solitude, but he embraced this next episode in his life with good humour and enthusiasm. In an effort to keep the family together he financed the purchase of a fishing boat for his two sons and played an active role in canvassing the authorities to build up the failing sea defences along the Suffolk coast to ensure there would not be a repeat of the devastating floods of his youth[92], when his family cottage at Old Beach was swamped by the sea as the coast of East Anglia was overwhelmed by a storm tide. The changing weather patterns of the last two decades of Thomas's life meant that flooding was becoming a seasonal occurrence.

Mindful that certain sections of the flood defences within the Suffolk estuaries were coming to the end of their current life, and that the threat of future global warming and rising sea levels may increase the risk of flooding if flood defences were not improved, Thomas looked at low cost solutions to help minimise the damage caused by flooding as well as high impact ways to avoid flooding.

Using the experience he gained as a boy in the floods of 1953, when communities worked together, Thomas galvanised local people to form a network of volunteers looking at ways householders could protect their homes from the effects of flooding[93]. By training a core group of volunteers, a scheme was set up to provide advice to local households so that they could carry out their own flood risk assessments on their homes. This involved

---

[92] The defence of existing land use patterns from encroachment by the sea is likely to become a more pressing issue as we move out to 2030. We have assumed that the weather has more storms and tidal surges which expose the vulnerability of coastal communities to flooding. We have also assumed a period of fiscal constraint, which limits the ability of the authorities to act to mitigate the flooding.

[93] We have assumed that, if the public authorities are unable to act to mitigate the flooding, local communities will act in their place. One of the benefits of this trend could be that greater community awareness develops over the next two decades. We have tried to capture this.

looking at the ways water could come into their home and assessing whether the perimeter walls of their house would be strong enough to take the expected weight of water should they be able to keep the water out. Collectively each community purchased smart air bricks which could be closed when the water levels rose, door protectors to keep the water out and heavy duty flood walls which could be used to block off an entire street during a flood[94].

At first these measures were seen by the community as an unnecessary expense until they realised how effective they were and the downward effect it would have on their insurance premiums[95]. He also canvassed local builders to build outdoor flood resilience into their new domestic and commercial developments incorporating porous surfacing materials such as gravel, small porous block paving and porous asphalt to allow surface water to drain away more easily.

On a larger scale, lack of public funding for adequate sea defences became another challenge for Thomas. Undeterred he set about raising the finance to build up the sea defences on a 30 miles stretch of the coast around Lowestoft. This was achieved through public subscription and grants from the Environment Agency over a 20 year period and proved its worth during the equinoctial storms and tidal surge in March 2026[96]. The sea defences around Lowestoft protected the town from the worst of the storm while

---

[94] We have assumed the continued development of smart building materials that can adapt to changing weather conditions. This, combined with a retro-fit of new materials to existing buildings, will provide a degree of protection against future flooding.

[95] We envisage quite an active role for the insurance sector in ensuring that flood defences are as good as they could be. We have assumed that the balance between the cost of protection and the benefit derived from additional insurance cover will be such that people are nudged towards securing their properties against flooding.

[96] We have assumed that, in an era of fiscal retrenchment, we see the return of public subscriptions as a means of funding social investment programmes. A pre-condition for this is the development of a sense of community to such a point that each individual within the community resists the temptation to enjoy the common benefits without making a contribution to their creation.

further down the coast many homes were destroyed as the coastline collapsed and the rivers flooded[97].

However, it may well be that Thomas will be most remembered for the vision and drive he exhibited in the latter part of his life. At the start of the 21st Century, he saw an opportunity for his family to capitalise on the burgeoning offshore wind farm industry that was growing apace off the coast of East Anglia, and at the same time give something back to the community[98]. By putting together an extensive business plan Thomas incorporated the wealth of knowledge that existed amongst the under-utilised skills of the local workforce to set up a community interest company[99]. With his organisational skills and ability to draw people together, it did not take long to build up a fleet of vessels, including a 14 metre rapid response vessel, and dominate the service cover to the expanding offshore wind energy farms that were being built in East Anglian waters.

Thomas felt confident that the emphasis placed on renewable energy by successive governments would mean that the industry would only go one way, and that was up. More off-shore wind farms would mean more work and it was not long before the company was employing a workforce of over twenty. In fact, this venture proved to be so successful that it funded another community interest company which was set up to install and run the off-shore wind turbines. This company not only produced free electricity for the benefit of the Waveney residents, it also created a financial surplus

---

[97] An inundation from the sea is a rather unpredictable event. We have assumed that the sea does not completely recede after this storm, and that it has the effect of permanently changing the coastline through the process of erosion and deposition.

[98] We have assumed that the off-shore wind industry, based around Lowestoft, provides a significant contribution to the regeneration of the lower Waveney Valley. Not only does it provide jobs directly, but also indirectly through the support services that the industry needs, and remotely through a local multiplier effect.

[99] We have assumed that altruistic people act in an altruistic fashion. We have assumed that, by 2030, there will be far more social enterprises in existence. Their mission is not only to make money but also to provide a service for the community in which they are based.

that enabled resources to be ploughed back into other community enterprises[100].

One such venture was to champion the provision of better facilities for the disabled. In 2012 the government sponsored work scheme where his daughter, Lily, had worked was closed down[101]. This left little, or no, opportunities for those with learning disabilities to earn a living. With Lily foremost in his mind Thomas set up a partnership focusing on people with disabilities and health conditions to make sure they were considered equally for jobs in the area. He spearheaded this initiative by working with the Coastal Wilderness Trust to set up an animal sanctuary which included rescuing injured seal pups, as these were Lily's favourite animal. The enterprise not only provided employment but also a tourist attraction bringing in much needed income to the area.

Following on from this, Thomas extended his work opportunity scheme to finding opportunities for young people in the area[102]. Experience had shown that Lowestoft was draining talent as the young people moved away to Ipswich or London to find work. By working with the local schools and businesses, Thomas was able to identify areas where apprenticeship schemes could be set up, particularly in the engineering and energy, port and logistics, and hospitality and catering sectors, all of which saw a surge of growth in and around Lowestoft in the latter years of his life.

---

[100] We have assumed that Thomas saw his role in life as one to serve his community. To him, the wind turbines owned and operated by the Community Interest Company were an asset belonging to the community and were there to provide a community facility – free electricity. This is a current trend that has the potential to develop much further in the years to come, especially if the supply of electricity becomes more uncertain and at greater cost.

[101] We have assumed that, owing to budgetary constraints, many social programmes would be closed in the years to 2030. Rather than allow a void to be created, we have assumed that individuals and community groups will step in to fill that void. In many respects, that is happening today. Our assumption is that it will be far more common by 2030.

[102] It is our view that one of the keys to regeneration is to halt the process whereby the most talented young people in Lowestoft leave the town because of a lack of opportunities. It is our view that this process needs to start at an early age by raising the aspirations of children at school and then by providing opportunities for young people to realise their aspirations.

One thing Thomas never lacked was energy. Many found it difficult to keep up with his abundant enthusiasm and zest for life and time and again his nickname of Bountiful Blowers proved itself to be true. Thomas had the ability to bring out the best in people which resulted in a wealth that could never be measured in money terms[103]. Two such examples of his bounty occurred after the storm of 2026 when the community interest company was awarded the contract to repair the wind turbines damaged by the storm and the decimation of the seal population meant that the seal sanctuary received a deluge of funding from concerned nature lovers as pictures of dying and injured seal pups were screened into homes across the country.

Thomas's energy and drive did not diminish with age but perhaps it waned a little when Poppy passed away in 2028. His legacy of hope and prosperity will no doubt continue through his family and the many thousands of people who have benefitted from his initiatives. He leaves behind three children, five grandchildren and a 'bountiful' community of friends.

---

[103] We have assumed that, by 2030, a degree of social change has taken place where the contribution of a person to society is no longer measured by how much money they have accumulated, but by how much they have contributed to their community.

Walking Round In Circles

Sometimes I feel as though I am walking round in circles and no matter how hard I try, I just cannot get out of it.

"You OK, love?" Ty asks.

I try to reassure him with a smile but when the sign for The Magistrates' Court appears in front of me, my head starts to spin. Ty gently takes my arm and guides me up the stairs to the thick glass doors, every inch of my body screaming for me to run and hide, but where would I go?   Suppose I could get Ty to make an excuse for me, tell the Magistrate I'm too ill to attend Court, yes that's what I'll do.

"Come on, Leigha, the sooner we get this over the better."

Before I can turn around Ty has put his arm around my waist and guided me through the automatic doors where a uniformed guard points us towards a scanner[104]. Ty nudges me forward.

"Look straight ahead and don't blink," the guard orders.

As I look at the camera my legs start to buckle but when Ty slips his calloused hand into mine I picture him out in his boat struggling to haul in nets of fish and know I must stay strong. I stare into the blue screen. God I hate these iris scanners[105]. You think by now they could have developed

---

[104] We have assumed that there will be a greater emphasis upon security in public buildings in the years to 2030. In this case, one has to verify one's identity just to enter the building. Exactly how this data is collected and by whom it is used is left to the imagination of the reader.

[105] We have assumed that the key aspect of identity verification in 2030 will be of a biometric form. We currently are witnessing the early stages of iris scanning as a way of

one which didn't make you go blind when it scanned you. Thank goodness I have Ty to support me.

"You're registered for Court Number Two. Down the hall, second set of chairs on the right. Move along now, I haven't got all day. Next."

"Come on love," Ty says ushering me away before I have a chance to remonstrate with the guard. He knows I have a quick tongue.

To be honest I blame that tight fisted madam at the dress shop for my present predicament. If she had not been so quick to call the Police I would not be here now. I offered to give the dress back but she would have none of it, said I couldn't give it back as it wasn't mine to give in the first place. Pleading with her made no difference. I explained my daughter needed a dress for her school prom at the end of the week as she had nothing to wear[106]. Even when one of the other customers said she would buy the dress for me it made no difference, the bitch just pointed to the sign over the door stating that all shoplifters would be prosecuted. She said it was happening all too often and an example needed to be set[107]. Now I feel as though all the stuffing has been knocked out of me. It's as though I'm being punished for something over which I have no control. Bethany needed a dress for her prom and I had no money to buy it. What was I to do? What makes it worse is that the last time I was in the Magistrate's Court for taking a dress for Megan's prom, I promised not to shoplift again. You think I would have learned my lesson, but no, I'm caught in that never ending

---

verifying a person's identity. By 2030, we have assumed that this technology will be almost ubiquitous, and will be used in many settings.

[106] We have assumed that the pressure upon parents to provide fashionable clothes for their children so that they can keep face with their peers will not have abated by 2030. It remains an issue of how parents without the means can afford to help their children in this way.

[107] Although the narrator has little sympathy with the shopkeeper, we must remember that if thefts are quite common, there is always more than one point of view to account for. When there is a general absence of prosperity, these social tensions will be abrasive on occasion. We see this lack of socialisation as a feature of our dystopian futures.

circle of despair. Now I could end up in prison. Suddenly the urge to go to the bathroom becomes overpowering, I tug on Ty's sleeve.

"Come on let's go and find the toilet," he says.

That's what I love about Ty, he knows exactly what I'm thinking. We've been together through thick, and now thin, for over 20 years. Not a bad innings seeing as how most of my friends have had several kids and each one of their fathers disappeared once the fishing dried up[108]. The thought that I might be parted from Ty and the girls makes my stomach churn.

"Come on Ley, looks like it's just down the corridor."

To my relief the washroom is empty and coming out of the cubicle I rummage in my handbag to find my water usage card[109]. Damn nuisance all these cards, my purse is now so big I have to tie an elastic band around it to keep them all from falling out. After swiping the sensor with my card, a stream of water flows out of the tap and, cupping my hands together, I splash it onto my face before the water dries up. Since the onset of water rationing I have become much more adroit in my water usage. However, when I look into the mirror I realise my mistake, as the make-up so carefully applied this morning has run down my face making me look like a washed out panda with black smudges round my eyes.

"Ley, you've been called."

---

[108] We have assumed a causal link between the lack of prosperity in a community and the degree to which it breaks down. In many respects, it then becomes a cycle that is hard to break free from. This is a key assumption in this scenario.

[109] We have assumed that potable water will be scarcer in 2030 than it is now and that a form of rationing will be in place to limit its use. We have envisaged a system where the rations are controlled electronically and can be accessed through the use of a swipe card. The swipe card then monitors usage and prevents access when the daily ration has been exceeded.

Ty's voice makes me jump and my handbag slips through my fingers onto the floor where the contents spill everywhere.

"We can sort this out later," Ty says as he rushes in and scoops everything back into the bag. "We need to get a move on."

In an effort to calm my nerves I breathe in deeply, close my eyes and as I exhale, open them again and look up into Ty's face. He smiles back at me.

"We'll be OK, love, I've just been speaking to your solicitor and he said we should be able to get you community service,[110]" Ty says as he wipes the smudges from my face. "Come on we've been in worse scrapes than this, let's get this over with."

As the hearing gets under way I try to work out where it all went wrong. I suppose my life started to change about ten years ago when they built a huge wind farm off the coast of Southwold. The politicians said it would bring prosperity to the region and it did for some, but not for us. The problem is that the wind turbines provide an ideal breeding spot for seal colonies but the seals get first dibs at the fish and as a result the fish stocks are no longer viable for commercial fishing[111]. It was cute seeing seals pop up in the harbour at Orford where Ty kept his boat and the tourists loved it, but it was devastating for Ty. Gradually his daily catch got less and this,

---

[110] We have not made explicit how legal representation is operated in this scenario. We have assumed that a system will be in place for those people who cannot afford legal representation. We have also assumed that trial will continue to be conducted in person and not through a remote communications device.

[111] The long term consequences of developing large off-shore wind farms have yet to become evident. In this scenario, we have assumed that they disturb the balance of sea life locally by facilitating the expansion of the seal population. The impact of this is to further propel into decline the fishing industry off the Suffolk coast. We have also assumed that the wind farmers offer no adequate compensation to the fishing industry for the loss of their livelihood.

combined with the rising cost of environmental compliance and the ever increasing cost of fuel, meant it was not economical to take his boat out[112].

Ty did look at alternative uses for his boat, like converting it to pleasure cruising, but he got tangled in a web of environmental red tape and we did not have the money to employ a solicitor to help us work through it. Then a consortium of businessmen from the Midlands bought up a fleet of boats and beat him to it, so there did not seem much point[113]. Anyway the bank turned us down for a business loan so we had to rely solely on what I got from cooking and cleaning in the holiday homes in the village[114]. The cakes and preserves I sold from outside our cottage on the main street gave us a bit more cash, but still it was not enough to provide for a family. The final straw came when we were evicted from the house we had lived in all our married life due to rent arrears and ended up living in Saxmundham[115].

"Does the defendant have anything to say before I pass sentence?"

I looked up at the Magistrate sitting at the bench, then over to Ty and I wondered where we would end up.

---

[112] We have assumed not only a period of ever increasing scarcity, where the basic cost of materials continues to rise steeply, but also a period where the effects of the mitigation policies work in such a way to increase the operating costs of small businesses. We envisage a period where environmental compliance will become a significant cost to the fishing sector.

[113] We have assumed that commercial opportunities are still present in this scenario, but that the cost of entry to the market is so high that only very well capitalised businesses can afford the initial start up overheads. This would create some employment locally, but the major portion of the prosperity attached to the business would be transferred out of the area.

[114] We have assumed that Suffolk – especially the Heritage Coast of Suffolk – becomes more a dormitory for Londoners and less of a coherent community in the years to 2030. Attracted by the beauty of the location, ever more people escape from the city by buying weekend cottages and holiday homes along the Suffolk coast. This has the effect of crowding out local people from the housing market.

[115] One of the effects of crowding out in the housing market is that the local population will move away from the places in which they have their roots. In this scenario, we have assumed the process to work through a combination of poverty and rent arrears. We have assumed that one of the effects of an influx of people onto the Suffolk coast is that residential rents have increased significantly.

"Your Worship, I can't guarantee what will happen in the future but I hate the fact I've sunk so low that I've had to steal to provide for my family and never want to be in that position again. My husband is out of work and there is little prospect of my children being able to afford to live in the village where they were born. I'll accept my punishment and do my best to escape from this downward spiral I now find myself in."

"Good for you, girl!" Ty shouted from the back of the Court.

"Silence," boomed the Magistrate, "or I will have you removed."

I felt as though I was going to be sick as I watched the Magistrate shuffle her notes.

"As this is not the first time you have appeared before this Court I am mindful to impose a custodial sentence[116]. However, taking into account the report from your solicitor and your determination to turn over a new leaf, I order you to undertake 200 hours community service. Report to the Clerk of the Court for direction."

It has been ten days since the court hearing and I have just completed my first day of community service. In many ways I wish I had been sent to prison as at least it would have been warm and dry, but I have since been told that due to over-crowding and the cost of incarceration there was little chance of that happening. Ty looked anxiously at me as I walked in the door.

"You must be frozen; it's not stopped raining all day. Come and sit down by the fire, I've just made a brew."

---

[116] We have assumed a reluctance to impose a custodial sentence owing to high levels of prison over-crowding. We envisage a continued use of community sentences as an alternative to incarceration, particularly on the grounds of cost.

I did not know whether Ty would laugh or cry when I told him which project the Coastal Wilderness Trust had me working on. You see they are setting up a seal sanctuary in Orford and need all the help they can get. Looks like Ty's dream of setting up a fishing boat again has gone forever.

CHAPTER 6

THE FOOD COMMUNITY

Food is likely to be a key issue out to 2030. Already long term food prices are rising as demand starts to outstrip supply. This could be a mixed blessing for Suffolk. As an agricultural county, Suffolk is well placed to benefit from the rising prices of agricultural produce. However, this benefit may not be shared generally as rising food prices squeeze the living standards of everyone and act as a tax upon consumption in general. This reduction in disposable income has the potential to keep the economy in Suffolk subdued for some time to come.

It is possible that disruptive climate change could start to become evident within the next twenty years. Rainfall could become more extreme, whilst long periods where no rain falls also become manifest. There are those who argue that we are already seeing this changing weather pattern, and warn that it could become even more extreme in the years to come. This may change our ability to produce food within the county. In turn, it could have major implications for the water infrastructure that is needed to irrigate the crops grown.

It is also expected that the impact of peak oil could start to become evident within the next twenty years. The disruptions caused to the food distribution system resulting from peak oil could mean that food is not necessarily delivered to market in a timely manner, and that the possible cost of food storage could become an issue by 2030. As much of agriculture is now dependent upon products derived from oil, the possibility of the increased cost of oil is likely to have the effect of increasing the cost base of farming.

How the balance of increased crop prices and increased input costs will play upon the farming community is largely uncertain at the moment. What is more evident is that the price of food paid by consumers is set to increase. This could have all sorts of consequences, but is likely to impact upon patterns of rural crime within the county. Just as the proceeds of crime increase in value, the ability of rural policing efforts to deal with those crime patterns is set to diminish.

This is not a given future though. It is possible to act now to mitigate the more dystopian effects of this future. For example, we could encourage less waste in our consumption of food. Households could be encouraged to grow more of their own food. Communities could develop strategies of resilience to counter food poverty. There is a great deal of scope for social enterprises to act as an alternative distribution method for those in food poverty. The basic infrastructure is currently in place. It just has to be used to secure a better future.

We wanted our scenarios to capture this duality within the food community. As things stand, both great opportunities are presented by the future we envisage and great challenges are also likely to accompany that future. Our utopian scenario captures some of these opportunities and looks at how a better future can be created. Our dystopian scenario considers what the future might look like if we are unable to rise to that challenge.

Our utopian scenario starts with a personal tragedy. We used the tragedy as a catalyst for change in the lives of the characters. We wanted to catch the theme of rising costs and scarcity, and how a reversal to a less mechanised form of farming might be a way of coping with the twin challenges of climate change and peak oil. In the story, the family copes with these changes by helping to develop a more closely knit community. We see that as a key development that is needed if the rural communities in Suffolk are to develop resilience as the future unfolds. We have deliberately left out interventions from the public sector because we feel that we ought to look at how communities might develop capacity without help from public agencies. If public austerity continues into the next decade, this might not be an unrealistic assumption.

The dystopian scenario pays more attention to the prospect of changing weather patterns and how they will impact upon crop yields. In this scenario, not only does the weather change, it becomes far more unpredictable as the seasons start to change as well. We have included an overlay of energy scarcity because we wanted to really make the point about how changing weather patterns and the high cost of fuel both combined have the potential for a particularly disruptive future. Despite strong demand for agricultural produce, the farmer in the story is unable to gain from that demand owing to low crop yields and outmoded methods of production. One of the points touched upon in the story is how public services – in this case the police – are limited in their delivery by obstacles placed by the weather. The delivery of public services to rural areas could be an issue in the years to come if the infrastructure on which we currently depend is rendered unusable by changed weather patterns. As this is a dystopian scenario, we have assumed that the public agencies have failed to adequately prepare for this eventuality. Let us hope that this does not actually turn out to be the case.

It is quite likely that Suffolk will retain its rural character in the years to 2030. If the climate forecasts for the next twenty years are anywhere near accurate, then it is quite likely that there will be some profound changes to the weather patterns experienced, which will have an impact upon the ability of the food community to operate. If, in addition to this, energy markets become tighter, then a number of challenges will arise for the food community. These challenges have to potential to be very positive and very negative. Which future we experience will depend upon our ability to make the best from those challenges.

Chillingham Manor - The Never Ending Story

Sunday, 2 January 2028

I will never forgive myself for badgering Robert to come home early from London for our Bonfire Night party. It was his birthday and I had planned a surprise for him, delivery of a Chillingham bull and two heifers, a breed once so endangered the location of the herd was kept a secret[117]. As it turned out I was the one to get the surprise, of the worse possible kind. Perhaps Robert would still be with me now if I had not telephoned him while he was driving on the A11 that Friday night. The screech of his brakes and explosion of metal will haunt me forever. But life must continue, at least that's what everyone tells me. No doubt they are right. Somehow I managed to get through the funeral and Christmas but now I must think of the future. With three children who depend on me and no money coming in, changes have to be made. I've either got to sell the manor or make the land work for us. The question is, how?

Sunday, 16 April 2028

"Happy Easter, Mummy," the children cried as they bundled through the bedroom door. "We thought you'd like breakfast in bed, just like you and Daddy used to do on Sunday morning," Felicity said as she lifted the red checked tea towel to reveal poached eggs on toast. "Brad and Jess collected the eggs this morning when they let the hens out."

Tears welled up in my eyes. Felicity had been wonderful over the last three months, taking charge of her two younger siblings while I tried to work out how to earn a living and cut our expenses. Taking the children out of boarding school and moving them to local schools had been a difficult

---

[117] We have assumed that the Chillingham remains a rare breed and that it has flourished in the years to 2030. We have also assumed that there is a premium to rare breeds, along with a desire to maintain them and rear them.

choice[118], especially for Bradley who had to move up into High School and missed playing rugby, but there was no option. The school fees were crippling.

"I've arranged for us to meet with Dan this morning," Felicity said sitting on the bed, crossing her legs. "We're lucky to have him. He knows so much about farming and his family have been breeding Suffolk Punch horses for generations."

Felicity, bless her, ever the optimist just like her father was.

"I've been thinking. Once I've done my GCSEs I'm going to college in Newmarket to learn about farm management, I want to set up a breeding programme[119]. Dan has confirmed that both cows are in calf so we should have two new additions by this time next year, all we need now are a few horses. Dan wants to bring his Suffolk Punch colt, Chillingham Boy, onto our farm, so that could start us off. Did you know his sire won best of breed at The Suffolk Show last year?[120]"

I tucked into my breakfast giving Felicity free rein to continue telling me her plans. It was hard to believe she had just turned 16 but her enthusiasm was contagious and a glimmer of excitement washed through me, perhaps she was on to something. Only last week I'd read an article about Thetford Forest using horses to clear the trees and with the cost of fuel escalating

---

[118] We have assumed that those with the means will continue to send their children to private schools. It could be argued that this education option may be closed by 2030, but we feel that it is a reasonable assumption that it will continue.

[119] We have assumed that farming will be more labour intensive than at present, and that there will be a revival in the bloodstock of horses for working the land. In many respects, this represents a rolling back of the rural technological paradigm.

[120] The Suffolk Show is the county show that has been in operation since 1831. We have assumed that it will continue until 2030 and beyond. It provides a venue for the various communities in rural Suffolk to meet, exchange ideas, and display their best animals and produce. It is likely to receive a boost in the scenario we currently envisage.

there were plenty of people looking at ways to become self sufficient[121]. Perhaps I should meet with Dan, after all what have I got to lose?

Thursday, 10 August 2028

Thank goodness I followed Felicity's advice four months ago and met with Dan, it's amazing what can be achieved in a short space of time. His suggestion to approach the Community Enterprise Scheme for a loan to renovate the barns was brilliant. Giving them a 10% stake in the farm was worth it as now I have a vision of where I want the farm to go[122]. From their input we've come up with a two pronged approach. On the one hand there is the breeding programme and on the other, a not for profit social enterprise programme, including a community farm and food project focusing on education and training[123]. We've decided to concentrate on setting up the community farm this year and Jedd, from Alternative Farming Solutions, has given me the names of people eager to be involved. We've set up a company limited by guarantee and at our first meeting signed up thirty members with a promise to Felicity that once she is 18 she can put herself forward to become a director. In the meantime I've rented out a parcel of land to the adjacent farm and earmarked a 20 acre site to start the community farm off. The rent from the land has provided funds to purchase our first poly tunnel and the cash injection from the new members has given us money to buy stock.

---

[121] Horses are currently used in some forestry operations in England. They provide a better transport option than tractors because they disturb the woodland floor less and they can get to parts of a wood that tractors would find too difficult. If we add to this the cost of escalating fuel, then the commercial viability of horses in forestry operations becomes more pronounced.

[122] An important part of the scheme we envisage to regenerate rural life would be a form of co-ownership and co-production. In this case, the Community Enterprise Scheme has provided funding and expertise in renovating the barn in return for a 10% stake in the equity of the farm. We suspect that banks may still continue to restrict lending in the years to 2030, thus creating an incentive for novel funding vehicles.

[123] Community farms already exist. We have assumed that they will be more common by 2030, as a way to rejuvenate rural areas. We envisage that they will be operated by people who live in towns and villages as a means to respond to the increased cost of food and a desire for a more simple lifestyle.

In June we started the pig club when eight beautiful weaners were delivered to the farm with a flurry of excitement and Jedd invited us to take part in his exciting project to extract biofuel from trees. I don't quite understand how it works, but apparently an enzyme converts carbohydrates into hydrocarbons to produce a hydrocarbon sap which can be harvested and converted for use as fuel[124]. All you need to process it is a small converter box, Jedd reckons that in time every household will have one. Whether it will work, only time will tell as it takes at least 15 years before the sap can be harvested, so I guess I'm in this for the long term.

Sunday, 1 April 2029

"Happy Easter Mummy," Felicity cried as she pulled back the curtains. "You'll never guess? Our herd has doubled overnight. We are now the proud owners of two Chillingham calves. You'll be pleased to know that mothers and babies are doing well, thanks to Dan's father who delivered them.[125]"

What a lot has happened in a year. Firstly there is no breakfast in bed this Easter and secondly Felicity has turned out to be quite the business woman. In fact she and Dan make a formidable pair. Dan still has his job as a night watchman at The Innovation Centre in Mildenhall as we can't yet pay him a wage, but we can offer him rent free accommodation so he has brought his colt over and moved himself into the flat above the stables. Felicity has started at college and has already made good use of her time by organising a student working party to tidy up the ménage. Just as well we don't have anyone living close by, their music kept me awake all night.

---

[124] The west of Suffolk is well placed to benefit from developments in the science of biofuels. Land is plentiful and is located close to the research centres at the University of Cambridge and the University of East Anglia. In this example, we are speculating upon the use of sugars within a plant to provide a fuel that could be used for transportation.

[125] An important part of rural life is the personal relationships that make rural society work. We have assumed that these relationships are as important in 2030 as they are today. Not only are people able to help each other, they are also willing to do so. In this regard, there is a high degree of social capital that binds rural society.

"Can't stay long," Felicity continued, "I've got to muck out the stables. We've got our fifth livery arriving today and I want to make sure the yard is tidy, especially as Dan held a painting party in his flat yesterday and goodness knows what mess his friends left behind."

Thank goodness for Dan and his contacts. The loan we received from the Community Enterprise Scheme enabled us to convert the old piggery into a kitchen and the adjoining barn into a workshop to hire out for social and educational functions, complete with disabled access. By next summer the dairy will be converted into a community cafe where we can use our produce and hold cookery demonstrations. After that we'll renovate the mushroom house for rent as a craft workshop. If we did not have Dan's endless network of labour, none of this would have been possible.

"You do realise," Felicity said, "that now the buildings are habitable and you've got all the health and safety and DBS checks with the Council, there's nothing stopping you from having your first educational visit. Dan has finished building the pens for the rabbits and guinea pigs and two new chicken coops."

Felicity is right. I've booked two schools to bring their Year Six pupils as part of their PSHE programme[126], one of them being Jessica's school. In fact it was Jessica's Year Six teacher who suggested I approach the Head as the school had been given a failing Ofsted report. When I told her that our workshops covering healthy lifestyles, community participation, enterprise and sustainable futures would fit in well with their Personal, Social, Health and Economic education programme, she looked physically relieved.

"Better go now," Felicity said pulling down the window letting the fresh spring air wash through the room, "the cows are lowing. Catch you later."

---

[126] We have assumed that Personal, Social, Health, and Economic (PSHE) education continues to 2030. We have also assumed the continued operation of Ofsted – a school standards inspectorate of Central Government – which will continue to grade the level of education delivered by an individual school.

Tuesday, 1st January 2030

What a journey these last two years have been since Robert was taken so dramatically from me. Success has been tinged with regret that he never got to see his Chillingham herd win best of breed at The Suffolk Show last year, though he would be proud of his family, especially Felicity. I doubt he would recognise her as the girl who was always in trouble at school with the self assured young woman who announced her engagement to Dan at the community farm's New Year's Eve party last night. Though there is a proviso. The wedding will not take place until The Orangery has been converted into a 100 seat wedding venue, Felicity is planning a big wedding, but that is a whole new story.

An Ill Wind

It was not so much the cold that depressed Tom, rather the fact that the winter had gone on for so long[127]. Here it was, Maundy Thursday, 18 April 2030, and Tom had emerged, bleary eyed, from the lambing shed to find yet another blizzard blowing drifts of snow across the roads making them impassable. This freeze was unexpected. He had already lost six lambs and a number of piglets and only two weeks ago, after a month of near solid rain, a flood had washed away the bridge linking the farm to the outside world. Bridge Farm had never felt so cut off.

"Come on Tom," Angela said, "sit down by the fire and have a cup of tea. You'll kill yourself if you don't slow down."

Tom was worried that if he stopped he would not have the energy to get up again, it had been a long night taking delivery of twenty lambs and he felt the energy draining from him. Standing in front of the fire feeling its warmth seep through his damp trousers reinforced this. If it wasn't for the wood burning stove they would have no heat as the oil for the central heating system had run out a week ago and even if supplies could have got through, they did not have the money to refill the tank[128].

"I've been going through the accounts for the farm and it doesn't look good," Angela said handing Tom a mug of tea. "I think we were lulled into a false sense of security last spring when the early wheat and barley crops gave us a bumper yield. Of course we were not to know the dry spell would carry

---

[127] One peculiarity of global warming is that it could well make winters in Suffolk much colder than previously experienced. The climate model that does this removes the benefit of the Gulf Stream through the de-salination of the Northern Atlantic, with the result that winters in Suffolk revert to the latitudinal mean (Suffolk is on similar latitudes to Alaska and Siberia).

[128] We have assumed that the background to rural life is one in which incomes are challenged by rising costs, input scarcities, and a lack of investment in rural infrastructure. Whilst the prices for food are rising, the difficulty in bringing produce to market on time does limit prosperity in the rural community.

on for so long leading to water restrictions, decimating our summer crops."

Tom pulled up his favourite chair and cupped the mug in his hands, its warmth bringing sensation back to his fingers. Sitting by the stove it was hard to remember the heat of last summer when it became so dry that even the slightest breeze would result in a dust cloud covering everything in a fine grit.

"If only the weather was more predictable, we could have used the money to pay off some of our bills rather than investing in a new harvester. What use is machinery after an autumn of near constant rain when even the smallest of tractors ends up stuck in the mud? Do you remember how we laughed when Jim, from Home Farm, divided up his fields ten years ago and planted hazel and hawthorn hedges and then bought a couple horses to plough his fields? Perhaps we should have listened to his advice and reduced the size of our fields to stop some of the soil erosion.[129]"

Tom drained his mug of tea and handed it back to his wife. The trouble was there was so much conflicting advice, primarily from Government agencies encouraging increased production to help feed the growing population. For years Tom had followed the advice of the experts and used the latest chemical fertilisers but when the agrochemical guys came to assess the land last year, they found that some of the fields were phosphorus deficient resulting in poor root development while others contained an excess of nitrogen resulting in poor plant quality and susceptibility to pests and disease. This imbalance resulted in reduced crop yields. No wonder the farm was losing money. It was even more galling when the neighbouring farms had diversified to organic farming in order to keep up with demand

---

[129] We have assumed that one of the impacts of a more extreme climate will be greater soil erosion as a result of a windier climate and more intense rainfall. We have also assumed that the official advice to the farming community will be a continued reliance upon fertilisers to increase yields. The scenario explores what could happen when these two trends collide.

from local food retailers, and were thriving on it[130]. The population explosion in East Suffolk, as people moved into the county to set up businesses, ensured their success as they brought with them the demand for a more varied and exotic diet. These aspirational types annoyed Tom immensely, demanding locally sourced produce and expecting their energy to come from renewable resources. What did they know about the land and how to work it[131]?

"Look, Tom, we've been through worse scrapes than this before," Angela said gently cradling her husband's face and giving him a kiss on his balding head, "at least December provided a respite and we managed to lift the sugar beet harvest and drill for winter wheat and spring barley. So what if the New Year came roaring in with a vengeance? We survived the four weeks in January when everything froze; even the salty waters along the estuary came to a standstill. OK, it took all our energy just to see to the animals and to keep the farm running, but we pulled together despite putting our life on hold."

Tom forced himself out of the chair, it would be so easy to stay in the warmth and block out the world around him. His head seemed to be in a constant fog, moving mechanically from one task to another, if someone offered him a realistic price for the farm he would take it. It would break his heart but the children had all moved away and were not interested in farming and he could not afford to take on permanent help. Last summer had been good though especially when a group of Italian migrant workers

---

[130] We have assumed that not all farmers have relied upon the existing paradigm for farming. Those who moved towards a more organic and small scale organisation are likely to do well as climate change starts to become apparent and as oil based resources start to become more scarce. We have assumed an inherent resilience in these operational structures.

[131] We have assumed that Suffolk continues to experience an influx of residents from London and South East England. What we are hinting at is a source of tension between the newcomers and those born in Suffolk as the newcomers bring with them a more urbane set of tastes in food. Those who can adapt to these changing tastes will thrive, fostering resentment in those who cannot adapt to change.

had knocked on his door looking for work[132]. He could not offer them money but they were happy to take up his offer of a piece of land to set up camp and a hot meal each day in exchange for a day's work each week. The rest of the week they worked in the surrounding area where their labour was in demand from the labour intensive farms. The Italians were good workers and Tom was sad when the harvest was over and they moved on to the Midlands when the work dried up, but at least Lorenzo stayed on, mainly due to the fact he had fallen for a young girl in the village. The lad seemed happy enough when Tom offered him his son's old bedroom in exchange for helping out on the farm over the winter and it seemed Lorenzo could turn his hand to most things including teaming up with a gang of Romanian builders.

"Come on, Tom, let's get the morning chores out the way. Lorenzo must be starving by now and in need of breakfast. It's hard to believe that so many of his friends in Italy are choosing to work on the land because they cannot find jobs in their chosen profession. Even though he has a degree in engineering Lorenzo would prefer to do farm work and eventually return to his family in the Dolomites to take over the farm from his father."

Out in his tractor Tom knew he should count his blessings, but it was hard when the wind kept blowing the snow against the cab window and fogging it up. In an effort to preserve his dwindling supply of diesel Tom did not turn on the heating system, for even if he had the credit to replenish it, it would be sometime before a delivery truck could get through to the farm[133]. The pigs needed feeding and the only way to transport it out to them was by tractor but as he drew up to Meadow Field the engine began to splutter.

---

[132] We have assumed that the United Kingdom remains a member of the European Union, with continued movement of labour between member states. We have also assumed that Italy continues to suffer within the Eurozone, and that young Italians continue to search for opportunities abroad.

[133] In this scenario, we wanted to highlight that scarcity was not only a question of price, but also one of availability. We readily assume the availability of our basic commodities, but if that infrastructure is impaired through a combination of austerity and climate change, then delivering basics to their point of use becomes more of a challenge.

Tom tapped the fuel gauge hoping it was the cold affecting the reading but as the engine juddered and stopped, he knew it was not. He was out of fuel. Climbing out of the cab a gust of wind caught him off guard and Tom fell backwards into a snow drift where he lay for a moment and let his mind drift back to when his father handed over the management of farm to him. It was the proudest moment of Tom's life and he could not conceive of doing anything else. The cold soon brought him back to the present and through the smothered shriek of the wind, he heard shouting. Tom held his breath wondering if his imagination was playing tricks, until he heard his pigs squealing. Someone was trying to steal his animals[134].

Tom jumped up and trudged back to the cab where he reached for his shotgun and grabbed some cartridges. Through the swirling snow he could make out two hunched figures loading piglets into a trailer and decided the best course of action would be to make as much noise as possible in the hope that they would be scared off. Tom shot two rounds into the air before running into the field hollering and waving his arms above his head. Startled, the intruders dropped the piglets and ran to the tractor but before they could climb in Tom fired another shot over their heads[135]. Instead of getting into the cab the pair ran straight on, scrambled over the fence and across the adjacent field. Only when they were an indistinct blur did Tom feel confident that he had seen the intruders off and could see to his pigs. He shored up the gap in the fence made by the abandoned tractor, fed the pigs then climbed up into the cab and was amazed to find the code to start it written in big letters by the ignition button.

---

[134] We have assumed that if the price of food is rising, then the potential proceeds of rural crime will rise. If that is combined with difficulties in the authorities policing rural areas, lessening the probability of being caught, then there will be a corresponding rise in the incidence of rural crime.

[135] Implicit in this scenario is an assumption that if rural communities feel abandoned by the authorities, then they will be more inclined to take the law into their own hands. We normally assume that the police have the ability to respond to a report of a crime, but we wanted to touch upon what would happen if this assumption could not be made.

"Not a bad day's work eh, Tom?" Angela said as they sat down to eat their evening meal, "all animals accounted for and the use of a tractor until the Police can get out here to retrieve it.   Apparently Sergeant Corble said he was aware of a gang operating in the area but there was little that could be done at the moment as the force had used up most of their monthly fuel allocation and would only to respond to life threatening emergencies.[136]"

Tom had mixed emotions about the day's events. On the one hand he would not be able to relax, wondering whether the gang would return to reclaim their tractor. On the other he now had the use of full tank of diesel.   One thing was sure he and Lorenzo would make sure they remained vigilant over the next couple of nights, just in case the pair returned.

As Tom lay in bed beside his wife that night reliving the day's events he chuckled to himself, marvelling at how inept the pair was to make it so easy for someone else to use their machinery.

"What was it Dad used to say, Angela? 'It's an ill wind that blows nobody any good'. Well perhaps today I proved him wrong."

---

[136] We wanted to touch upon how the emergency services could operate in times of severe resource scarcity. We have assumed that there continues to be an insufficient emergency buffer in police budgets to cover significant rises in the cost of fuel, and that the police respond by limiting the use of fuel per month, as they did during the oil crisis of 1974.

CHAPTER 7

CONCLUSION

One of the principal beliefs expressed in this book is that, from the perspective of the present, the future is not fixed. In this respect it is possible to talk about many different possible futures that may or may not come to pass. The actual future that finally occurs is likely to be an amalgam of a large number of the possibilities that we currently can foresee.

This is an important point because in each of the scenarios we have presented a vision of how the future could be. In no sense are the scenarios predictions of the future. A prediction would establish a single future, which may either be right or wrong. An imagining of the future, as we have lain out in the scenarios, ought to be taken as a statement of possibility. It is an anticipation of future events under a very specific set of circumstances.

When setting out a series of scenarios, it is important to highlight some of the key assumptions that have been brought to those scenarios. The entire work is based upon two key assumptions. First, that in the year 2030, in England, we shall experience shortages of a number of key resources, the most pressing of which will be a shortage of energy. Second, that in the year 2030, we will still be experiencing the repercussions of the financial crisis through prolonged austerity in the provision of services by the public sector. We need to both justify the choice of these assumptions and to consider the possibility that they may be wrong. We will do this by examining each assumption in turn.

The concept of 'Peak Oil' is a shorthand expression of the view that resources – especially oil as a key resource – are being used at a pace that is faster than the supply of those resources can increase to accommodate that demand. There arises a situation where supply is tight and the cost of the

101

resources is relatively high and rising. This is a reasonable assumption when taking a long term perspective for a number of reasons.

Despite any short term abatements in the markets for commodities such as oil, the long term trends are towards tighter supply. A principal driver of this trend is the rising population across the globe. In the year 2000, global population was estimated to be 6 billion. The mid-range estimate of global population for the year 2050 is between 9 billion to 10 billion people, with most of the 50% rise being skewed towards the earlier part of this 50 year period. These additional people on the planet will need to be housed, fed, educated, and employed. Unless there is a dramatic reduction in living standards in the developed world, accommodating this increase in population is bound to increase the demand for resources. If supply is reasonably constrained by the finite planet on which we live, then it is not unreasonable to expect a period of resource scarcity, where the price of resources are on an upward trend.

This is not quite the end of the story. Not only are there likely to be more people occupying the planet, but it is also likely that their expectations of life will grow as well. The history of our recent past supports this argument. The recent history of the enrichment of China, for example, has demonstrated that as incomes rise, then the expectations of the population for food rise as well. Rising incomes are also associated with, for example, rising meat consumption. This will compound the impact of greater numbers by increasing the resource intensity of the global population. It is reasonable to assume that there will be more people consuming more resources per head by 2030. This is the assumption contained in the book. We can see elements of resource scarcity in all of our scenarios, but it is particularly marked in "Life's Not Fare – A Taxi Driver's Tale" and "An Ill Wind", where the sources of dystopia are the resource scarcities. Not all of the stories with resource scarcity are dystopic. We deliberately juxtaposed "An Ill Wind" with "Chillingham Manor" to demonstrate that a good outcome can be found within the parameters of resource scarcity and personal tragedy. The assumption about scarce resources could, however, be unfounded. In futures, it is normally the case that every trend has a counter-trend, and we need to think about the counter-trend to resource scarcity.

Historically, it has been the case that the scarcity of one particular resource has stimulated the development of a technology to mitigate the scarcity of that resource. To some extent, we have seen this effect already. A rising price of oil has stimulated, for example, the development of electric cars, using electricity as a power source instead of oil derivatives such as petrol or diesel. The vulnerability of our core assumption of resource scarcity is that we are also stating that there will be no rapid development and widespread use of alternative technologies to counter the resources which are scarce in the years to 2030. In many respects, this is almost a self-fulfilling prophecy. An essential part of the process by which new technologies are developed and funded is through the price mechanism. The high price of a commodity will make worthwhile the investment in developing a technology to economise its use. Oil at over $100 a barrel is more likely to stimulate electric cars than oil at under $50 a barrel. This theme is captured in "Bountiful Blowers" with the development of off-shore wind power as a source of energy; and "West Suffolk Creative Ltd" and "Chillingham Manor", a linked pair of scenarios, which touch upon the possibility of a biotech source of future energy.

We have allowed for some development and use of alternative technologies because to do so would be an unreasonable restriction. We have tried to pitch the scenarios at that point where the new technologies are emerging. They are not quite absent, but they are also not quite ubiquitous. It may turn out that we have struck the wrong balance in this, but we feel that we have the right balance for the present.

If the core assumption of a period of relative resource scarcity might raise eyebrows at present, the core assumption of continued austerity into the future might be considered to be unduly pessimistic in the present. Perhaps it is a more controversial assumption because it suggests that we are unlikely to see the return to the periods of prosperity that we experienced in the 'Great Moderation'. It may be helpful to outline why we used this as a core assumption, and why it may be that the assumption could turn out to be wrong.

The case for continued austerity in the public sector is a simple one of debt and deficit. From a long term perspective, the key driver of deficit is the rate at which the population in the UK is ageing. In the years to 2030, if mortality rates do not increase dramatically, there will be a substantial increase in the number of people who are over 65, and an even more dramatic increase in those aged over 80, in percentage terms. The Baby Boomers will, at first, retire, and then enter into a period of substantial frailty. As this happens, the pressure on the public purse will be considerable. The ageing population will increase the total spent upon pensions and healthcare, particularly as pensions in the UK are unfunded and as the delivery of healthcare in the UK is free at the point of use. We are likely to see the increase in the demand for adult social care as the population of the elderly becomes frailer and more vulnerable. Those trends are woven into the fabric of UK demographics out to 2030.

There are also a number of more pernicious trends at work to exacerbate this situation. If we first state the obvious, retired people work far less than people of working age. Indeed, the whole concept of retirement is based around the absence of employment. This shift in the balance of the population from the employed to the retired will reduce the income core from which income tax and national insurance (a form of employment tax) is levied. It is also the case that the spending habits of people at different life stages are different. After a spending binge immediately after retirement on items such as cruises, as people grow older and move from independent elderhood to dependent elderhood, they spend less. As this is likely to happen at some scale, one can also question the receipts from Value Added Tax (a sales tax) that will be derived in the years to 2030.

Putting this together, the assumption argues that not only is the spending base likely to increase to 2030, but also the tax base has the capacity to shrink. In the light of this, policy makers face three broad alternatives. One is to borrow more to maintain the level of public services. Another is to scale back the level of public provision in the hope that the private sector, either through familial help or through commercial provision, will take up the slack. The final possibility would be to offset the falling tax base by dramatically increasing the level of taxation. It is not unreasonable for policy to contain a blend of these three possibilities and for politics in the years to come to be about where that balance should be set. However, it is also not unreasonable to consider that an extended period of austerity may be evident out to 2030. We wanted to capture this as a trend in our pair of Caring Community scenarios – "Pavla & Raina Hinova" and "Lost In Time". The utopian scenario - "Pavla & Raina Hinova" – points to a possible way out through the immigration of young people, the public expenditure upon which is seen as a public investment. By way of contrast, the dystopian scenario, "Lost In Time", represents a continuation of austerity without any transformative counter-trends. In the one, austerity is mitigated, in the other it isn't.

And yet, it is also possible that this assumption of continued austerity could be misplaced. The key weakness to our assumption of continued austerity concerns labour productivity. Implicit in our assumption is that there is no significant increase in labour productivity in the year to 2030. If there were to be, then it would be entirely possible for fewer workers to produce an equal – or even greater - level of output. That would have the effect of shoring up the tax base which, in turn, would make greater levels of expenditure possible.

There are two broad ways of increasing labour productivity from a societal perspective. One is to change the balance between work and retirement, and the other is to enjoy the benefits of improvements in the technologies that allow a greater degree of labour productivity.

The assumption about continued austerity in the public sector presumes that the current relationship between work and retirement remains fixed. We know that this may not be entirely correct. Changes are currently being made to that relationship. The age at which one retires is gradually increasing, with the effect of retaining in the workforce larger numbers of people. It is also the case that many retirees wish to continue working. By and large they have their health, their pensions – particularly defined contribution pensions - may not be paying them quite as much as they hoped for, and they may miss the social contact that work provides. One trend that we are currently witnessing is the rise of the silver-haired workforce consisting of the independent elders. The twin effects of a rising retirement age along with the desire of those retired to continue working ought to ease the impact of austerity in the years to come.

The greater impact, however, ought to be felt from a renewed wave of technological development. Economic history tells us that technology tends to come along in waves. The last great wave was the information revolution, which started to be felt in the 1980s. If we consider how labour productivity has changed over the course of the last thirty years, we can see the potential of technology to revolutionise the way in which we work. The pace of technological advance has abated in recent years, and there are those who believe that this maturation process of the information revolution heralds the start of a renewed wave of technology.

We are, at present, unable to say for certain what the subject of that revolution will be. However, there are grounds to suspect that it will be to mitigate some of the problems highlighted in our scenarios. If we are to be faced with a period of relative resource scarcity, then technology offers a solution to our desire to get more output from less input. In doing so, it raises our productivity, which is the basis upon which prosperity is based. It could be that, in the years to 2030, we do witness a surge in new technologies with the effect of raising productivity and underpinning refreshed prosperity. If that happens, then we can expect the tax base to be revived. We wanted the utopian scenarios in the Creative Community ("West Suffolk Creative Ltd") and the Entrepreneurial Community ("Lucky Stars") to capture how innovation and the development of technology could become the basis of future prosperity. It also may be possible, if some of the new technologies are designed to help with the care of the elderly, that the pressure on the spending side of the equation is eased.

In our scenarios, the utopian set tends to include the possibility of technology and innovation providing a means to improve the lives of our fictional characters. It is important to note that new ways of doing things are just as important as the new technologies in the process of innovation. In some cases, just small changes in operating procedures, enabled by a new technology, can have a great impact in making better the lives of people. The dystopian set of scenarios tends to suggest that there is no great impact of new technologies in the year to 2030. The technologies are there, but have yet to become widely adopted and used. This reflects the presumption that Suffolk remains a community of late adopters of new technologies and improved working practices. This contrast is evident in the pair of scenarios for the Food Community. In the utopian scenario, "Chillingham Manor", new methods for rural prosperity are embraced. In the dystopian scenario, "An Ill Wind", they are resisted, with a consequence that the characters fail to achieve a meaningful level of prosperity.

As we can see, the scenario set relies upon two key assumptions that could reasonably be challenged. It is important to stress that the scenarios are outlines of future possibilities and do not represent predictions of the future. Although some might find the assumption of resource scarcity and continued austerity in the public sector unconvincing, within the boundaries of scenario creation, we thought that it would yield interesting results if those assumptions were to be made.

A further objection to the set of scenarios could be that we have made the right base assumptions, we have identified a convincing set of critical uncertainties, but we have considered the wrong communities. It is worth outlining why we have adopted the approach set out in this book. As can be seen above, a critical uncertainty revolves around the degree of prosperity Suffolk enjoys in the years to 2030. As this is such a core uncertainty, we felt that we had to lead with this issue.

The choice of communities – The Creative Community and the Entrepreneurial Community – was influenced by our belief that, in a modern economy, the creative industries are the key to the generation of prosperity, and the entrepreneurial community is the vehicle to deliver that prosperity. They are a matching pair. There is a degree of cross-over between the characters and situations described in the scenarios, which reinforces this point.

If growing prosperity allows the community to face the challenges ahead, then we felt that we ought to consider the communities in which the challenges might be felt. As we have already outlined, the sheer momentum of current demographics is such that Suffolk will age in the years to 2030. The degree of dependency that this ageing will call into being might be questioned, it really depends on how the balance between independent elderhood and dependent elderhood falls, but what cannot be questioned is that the population will age. This is why we decided to consider the Caring Community as a focus. It will be in this area that the greatest impact will be felt.

It is also the case that poverty and deprivation, as well as prosperity and affluence, are present throughout Suffolk. In geographical terms, the communities along the Suffolk coastline contain elements of both extremes.

If we were to consider the geographical impact of the scenarios, then the Coastal Community stands out as worthy of attention. Along the same lines, Suffolk is a rural county and the rural community also exhibits some of the extremes of deprivation and affluence. This thinking was behind our choice of the Food Community as the fifth community for which we prepared scenarios. We felt that the Coastal Community and Food Community together would give a broad scope to our work.

It could be objected that we have not included a great deal of the urban communities in Suffolk; that we have been partial in the aspects of the business community that we have found interesting; and that we have kept our focus away from the public services traditionally provided by the large public bodies within the county, such as health, education, and social services. This is all true. However, in a project such as this, we are unable to study every facet of the communities of the future and we decided to draw the line where it is drawn. We felt that it would be mistaken for us to align our work too closely to that of any of the current institutions who provide those services. Our work is not about the NHS in Suffolk or the work of Suffolk County Council. It is about the people of Suffolk and how they may live their lives over the next decade and a half.

This brings us full circle back to where we started. From the perspective of the present, the future isn't fixed. There is ample time for people to shape the future in which they live. The role of scenarios is to provide an imagining of how that future may develop. We could experience the joys of a utopian future just as much as sharing the challenges of a dystopian one. Either is possible here in the present. The set of scenarios are designed to inspire action to build a better future whilst also providing a warning about futures that we do not want to happen. It is up to us to create a better future. After all, we will all be living in it.

Acknowledgements

We would like to express our gratitude to those people who participated in the development of the project. In particular, we would like to thank the following for giving up their time to contribute to the development of the various scenarios.

Suzanne	Arnold	Liz	Harlaar	Tibbs	Pinter
Trazar	Astley-Reid	Ned	Harrison	Dilva	Porter
John	Bamford	Faith	Hicks	Nick	Price
Mark	Bermingham	Martin	Hine	Andy	Proctor
Mandy	Blunden	Andy	Hollingsworth	Jai	Raithatha
Nicola	Bradford	Andrew	Hunkin	Gary	Raynor
Steve	Butterworth	Richard	Hutchinson	Damien	Ribbans
Tim	Buxbaum	Rita	James	Sharon	Saunders
Ruth	Buxbaum	Emma	Jell	Gemma	Sayers
Theo	Clarke	Gladys	Jones	Allan	Scott
Paul	Daltry	Jason	Joseph	Toby	Slater Robins
James	Davey	Rosa	Juarez	Ana	Stanic
Alison	Donald	Jayne	Knight	Gavin	Talbot
Lucy	Drake	Emily	Manser	Sam	Thomas
Kathleen	Dunmore	Steve	Marsden	Gilly R	Thomson
Dawn	Easter	Kirsty	Martin	Rebecca	Turbitt
Steven	Emmerson	Julie	Mason	Janus	Van Helvert
John	Engbeck	Tim	Mason	David	Walton
Bob	Feltwell	Stuart	McCreery	Toby	Walton
Sarah	Fogarty	Veronique	Mermaz	Stephen	Watt
Alison	Fordham	Amelia	Moore	Esmee	Wilcox
Dan	Gaul	Guenever	Pachent	Kirsty	Wilmot
Charlotte	Glass	Bill	Parker	Nick	Wilson
Belinda	Godbold	Wendi	Pasco-McGregor	James	Wilson
Chris	Gordon	John	Patman	Nicholas	Woolley
David	Hales	Suzanna	Pickering		

We are also indebted to the large number of people who we consulted over the ideas expressed in the book for the advice and expertise which they gave us. We are grateful to those who gave an opinion on some of our ideas, and who provided us with a necessary feel for what would work in the scenarios and what would not. Any errors in the development of the scenarios are entirely of our own creation.

Stephen & Joanne Aguilar-Millan